COUNTRY LIFE
IN CLASSICAL TIMES

COUNTRY LIFE IN CLASSICAL TIMES

K. D. WHITE

Cornell University Press
Ithaca, New York

First published 1977 by Cornell University Press
Second printing 1979

International Standard Book Number 0-8014-1114-9
Library of Congress Catalog Card Number 77–74923

Printed in the United States of America

For Audrey and Olowo Ọjọade

CONTENTS

Chapter III The Country through the Eye of the Townsman   36

Chapter VII The Changing Patterns of Rural Life 84

Chapter VIII Rural Cults and Festivals 96

Chapter X Hunting and Fishing   118

PLATES

ACKNOWLEDGEMENTS

For use of the following illustrations we are indebted to: Plates 1, 5, 32, National Museum, Naples; Plates 2, 8, 9, Museum of Civilization, Rome; Plate 6, Alinari, Florence; Plates 7, 23, National Museum, Rome; Plates 10, 11, 19, Bardo Museum, Tunis; Plates 14, 20, 21, 22, Mansell Collection, London; Plate 15, Louvre, Paris; Plate 16, Landesmuseum, Trier; Plates 18, 31, Roger Wood, London; Plate 24, Vatican Library, Rome; Plates 26, 27, Cherchel Museum, Cherchel, Algeria; Plate 28, Fitzwilliam Museum, Cambridge; Plate 29, Italian State Tourist Office, London; Plate 30, Scala Istituto Fotografico Editoriali, Florence; Plate 33, National Museum, Madrid. Plate 3 is Crown copyright and reproduced with permission of the Controller of Her Majesty's Stationery Office, London

The following publishers have kindly given their permission for use of copyright material: Ernest Benn Ltd, from *A Literary History of Rome* by J. Wight Duff; Indiana University Press, from Rolfe Humphries' translation of Ovid's *Metamorphoses*; University of Michigan Press, from Richmond Lattimore's translation of Hesiod's *Works and Days*; Penguin Books Ltd, from Harold Isbell's translation of Rutilius Namatianus from *The Poets of Imperial Rome*, and from E. V. Rieu's translation of Homer's *Odyssey*; Yale University Press, from *Roman Social Relations* by Ramsay MacMullen.

2—CLICT • •

PREFACE

This is, I believe, the first anthology of its kind to appear in any language. The idea of composing it first occurred to me while working in Rome a decade and more ago, and enjoying for the first time the pictorial delights of the Vatican Virgil. I thought of it from its inception as a book in which the reader might hope to find among the illustrations a painting, a relief or a mosaic that caught the flavour of a particular passage of poetry or prose, and perhaps occasionally some appreciable degree of interplay, and even of integration, between scene and story, between the artist and the writer. Considerations of cost have made it impossible to include all the illustrations I had planned to use; but I have tried to make up for this by the references I have made to accessible works in which these may be found.

The extent of my indebtedness both to books and people is very great; in particular, the introductory essay owes much to Jacques André's illuminating studies of *otium*, Victor Ehrenberg's perceptive chapter on Attic farmers, Karl Schefold's masterly interpretations of 'sacro-idyllic' landscapes, and Ramsay MacMullen's downright comments on the seamy realities of country life under the Romans. Behind them stand two towering figures of former times, Heitland and Rostovtzeff—each a perennial fount of inspired comment on virtually every aspect of life in the countryside.

Personal obligations are also great: many friends and colleagues have helped both in the selection of material and in the making of the Introduction. I am particularly grateful to Nigel Henry, John Crook, Alan Cameron and Guy Lee; to the last-named also for his most generous contributions to the translations. It is a pleasure to acknowledge once again my debt to Ana Healey and her colleagues in the Library of the Institute of Classical Studies, London, for much bibliographical and other help at various stages in the preparation of the book. My sincere thanks are also due to the Vice-Chancellor of the University of Jos and his colleagues for calling back to the colours a veteran, *iam rude donatum*, and providing him with fresh opportunities for teaching and writing in the stimulating atmosphere of the Nigerian Plateau; to Mrs Iweriebor and Mr Eshiwe of the Department of Humanities at Jos, for bearing the brunt of the typing. My debt to my former pupil at Ibadan, Dr Ojoade, now Head of the Department at Jos, and to his versatile wife, is acknowledged elsewhere in the book.

K. D. White
Jos, December, 1976

I

INTRODUCTORY

Most books about daily life in Greece and Rome—and there is a wide range of good books to choose from—tell the reader a great deal about life in cities and towns, especially in Athens and Rome, with perhaps a chapter on agriculture and life on the farm. There are good reasons for this distribution and emphasis: the life of the cities, or rather, of a limited number of them, is well documented; that of the countryside is not. In the words of one of our leading authorities, 'the cities have told us their story, the country always remained silent and reserved'.[1] In gathering together this collection of translations from Greek and Roman writers I have sought to show that the countryside, in which the vast majority of the inhabitants of the Graeco-Roman world lived and worked, was not so inarticulate after all. If this book were a study of the English countryside and its inhabitants, the reader would doubtless expect to learn something about country speech, country dress and country manners, about markets and fairs and other traditional activities, about the status and relationships of landowners and their tenants, and of course about the cheque-book farmers, the jumped-up lords of the manor, and other recent arrivals on the contemporary rural scene.

Before attempting to indicate how many of these topics are relevant in the classical period, we must first look at the scope of our subject. If we were discussing city life, as opposed to country life, we should find our view severely restricted; in the case of Greece, we know very little about any city apart from Athens, while in that of Italy, thanks to the eruption of Vesuvius in A.D. 79, we know a great deal more about the daily life of the ordinary citizens of Pompeii and Herculaneum than we do about life in Rome. We must, however, bear in mind two compensating factors: the many hundreds of Greek city-states had many recognizable features in common,[2] and the provinces of the Roman Empire were well supplied with replicas of the Eternal City, large or small, each complete with Capitol, Temple of Jupiter, amphitheatre and forum.

To this partial uniformity the countryside and its inhabitants stand in sharp contrast. Looking at them means looking at life in areas as different in racial and cultural background and social organization as Britain or Gaul on the one hand, and Syria or Egypt on the other. So we must be on our guard against the temptation to universalize from a single reference. Another difficulty arises from the strongly urban-oriented bias of our sources. Civilized life was in classical antiquity concentrated in the cities: and for those who lived in a Greek *polis* or a Roman *urbs* the country folk (*georgoi/cultores, agroikoi/agrestes, kometai/pagani*) were part of an inferior order. Most of the information that comes our way about country folk and country life reaches us at second-hand, from the pens of city-dwellers; only here and there do we seem to catch the authentic note of the country, undistorted by prejudice or propaganda. To many city folk the rustic was, as in many other periods of history, a figure of fun, a bumpkin, an obvious target for ridicule, as in bourgeois comedy.[3] By others he was used as a conventional figure, either as a foil for satirists and philosophers engaged in pointing the contrast between rustic virtues and city vices, or, at a further remove from reality, in the shape of the 'idyllic' rustic swain of pastoral poetry.

Most of these country types, whether buffoons, or heroes or cardboard shepherds, are as conventional as the landscapes that adorned the walls of elegant town houses in Pompeii, or Herculaneum. Occasionally we get a more direct view of country life. The rustic heroes of Aristophanes' wartime comedies, such as the farmer Dikaiopolis in the *Acharnians*, or the vine-dresser Trygaios in the *Peace*, have a down-to-earth quality that springs from direct observation, with the appropriate attributes of coarse wit and homespun humour (see Ch. VIII a). The tenants of the great Roman landowners, whether private or imperial, are not very articulate, but the Younger Pliny, who was genuinely, if paternalistically, interested in the people who provided him with his income, does give casual glimpses of the realities of life on the land at the end of the first century A.D.[4] Surviving inscriptions, too, show some of the ways in which imperial tenants were exploited by the servants of their imperial masters.[5] The majority of those who worked on the land were peasant farmers; authentic descriptions of their work are scarce, but revealing. Pride of place goes to a remarkable poem, the *Works and Days* of Hesiod, who farmed the hard way in the stony foothills of Mount Helicon, battling against the harsh extremes of torrid summers and ice-cold winters.[6] Apart from this substantial contribution from early Greece, we have little else in the way of direct description; there are a few fleeting glimpses in Virgil's *Georgics*, and a brief, but detailed and authentic, account of the beginning of a day on a small farm by an anonymous contemporary of Virgil, the poem known as the *Country Salad* (*Moretum*) (Ch. I m).

Most classical literature was written for upper-class readers by writers who either were upper class by birth, or had acquired the mores and the outlook of those for whom they wrote. This limitation applies as much to the technical sphere as to that of general literature: the agricultural handbooks of Cato, Varro and Columella are addressed, not to peasants, but to 'gentleman farmers', the absentee owners of plantations or ranches; and, like Virgil's *Georgics*, they will have been perused by men with literary inclinations who enjoyed little or no contact with the daily routines of life on the land. The patterns of relationship between townsmen and country folk were as diverse and as historically variable as they are today, containing some elements that are familiar, and others for which no parallels exist in our contemporary world.

As a starting-point I take a well-known passage from the *Histories* of Tacitus,

2

in which the Roman historian, after briefly reviewing the condition of the various provinces and dependencies of the Roman Empire at the beginning of the disastrous civil wars that followed the death of the emperor Nero, rounds off his survey with a few remarks about Egypt:

> Egypt, together with the troops to control it, had been governed since the time of the deified Augustus by Roman Knights who replaced the former kings. It had seemed sensible by this means to keep under the direct control of the imperial house a province which is difficult of access, with an abundant production of corn, but disorderly and unstable by reason of the fanatical superstition of the inhabitants, who are both strangers to law and unacquainted with magistrates. (11.84)

A number of points in this passage call for comment: 'difficult of access' refers to the strategic situation of the region; the only feasible approach by land is across the Sinai peninsula, and a force invading by sea could not approach unobserved. Our concern, however, is not with strategic problems, but rather with the attitude reflected in the reference to the common people of the territory. The adjectives used to describe the subject population are pejorative, sweeping and dismissive, and their tone is unmistakable: it is that all too familiar one of imperious contempt for the 'lesser breeds without the law'.[7] This attitude of superiority was not however peculiar to this particular sphere of human relations: examples abound outside the imperial ruler-subject relationship; but the Egyptians receive a full charge of it because they are doubly contemptible: they are not only bottom-dogs, living at the base of the social pyramid of a highly stratified society; they suffer from the additional disadvantage of being *peasants*. This brings us to our most important relationship, that between townsman and countryman, *rusticus* and *urbanus*, *agroikos* and *polites*.

The deep cleavages of outlook and the mutually hostile elements in this relationship, or rather bundle of relationships, are masked to some extent in our modern terminology; words like 'urbane' and 'polite' have been completely divorced from their originally divisive contexts, and the words 'boor' and 'boorish' have almost completely lost their rustic associations; the word 'peasant' has only recently acquired a non-rustic connotation. But we need only glance at Theophrastus' character sketch *The boor* (Ch. I e), or young Nasica's encounter with the rustic voter (Ch. I j), to feel the impact.

At the same time, we must remember that townsmen and country folk were not divided politically as they have been in England since the Industrial Revolution. Thus the *ekklesia*, the popular Assembly that was the sovereign body at Athens, was composed of both townsmen and countrymen: 'When the voters who had elected bad officials are cursed, the words of the curse are: "neither shall their cattle produce offspring, nor their soil bear crops". This . . . would be nonsense if the majority of the people in the *ekklesia* were only townsfolk, as is generally believed. They were peasants as well.'[8] The point emerges very clearly from a passage in the Athenian historian Thucydides. At the beginning of the Great War between Athens and Sparta (431–404 B.C.), all Athenian citizens and their families living in the countryside were evacuated, and lodged in Athens, as an essential part of the overall strategy of Perikles, which was to avoid land battles, and concentrate on seapower—in which Athens had a great advantage. This meant a massive uprooting for the majority of the population, as the historian is at pains to point out:

> The Athenians took the advice he gave them, and brought in from the country their wives and children and all their houses ... Their sheep and cattle they sent across to ... offshore islands. But the evacuation was a difficult experience, since the majority had always been used to living in the countryside ... (11.14)

He then gives a brief account of the early history of the region before its unification, when the territory had been divided into independent states. Even after unification, he points out, old habits persisted, most Athenians, right up to his own time, being born and bred in the countryside:

> So they were far from happy at being uprooted with their entire households ... it was with sadness and reluctance that they now abandoned their homes ... and prepared to alter their whole way of life, leaving behind what each man regarded as his own city. When they reached Athens, a few had houses of their own to go to, and a few were able to find shelter with friends or relatives; but the majority had to settle down in those parts of the city that had not been built over, and in the temples and all the shrines of the heroes, except the acropolis. 11.16–17)

The most striking feature of this account is what it tells us about the relationship between the majority of the citizens of the Athenian state and their city. It would seem that for most Athenians their city was more like what in England is known as a 'country town' rather than a city—that is, a centre to which the inhabitants of the villages, hamlets or isolated farms of the neighbourhood resort to sell their surplus produce and buy what they need, as well as to participate in various communal activities, political, cultural or religious.[9]

The rural hinterland also set a distinctive stamp upon the individual citizen. The territory of fifth-century Athens was divided up into regional sections known as *demes*. When a male Athenian 'came of age', he was enrolled as a member of his *deme* by a ceremony of admission, and it was this that gave him his badge of citizenship; henceforth he was known in the official records as so-and-so, son of so-and-so, of the *deme* so-and-so; thus the famous statesman Demosthenes appears in official records as Demosthenes, son of Demosthenes, of the *deme* Paiane. Roman citizens were also enrolled in territorial divisions called 'thirds' (*tribus*). Group-voting in these 'tribal' divisions was the basis of the organization of the legislative assemblies, and the territorial implications of citizenship played a very important part in the politics of the Roman Republic, especially where new citizens were being enrolled on the 'tribal' registers, and political pressures were applied to increase or decrease the relative importance of 'city' and 'country' votes. The Roman state at its fullest extent had thirty-five

4

voting districts, but only four of these lay in the city itself; the other thirty-one lay outside. As Rome expanded her power, she incorporated part of the territories of her defeated neighbours, settling her own citizens on these parcels of land, and it was these lands that gave them their voting rights. As time went on, the parcels of land available for distribution were moved further and further away from Rome. Some of her remotest citizens had to travel as much as sixty miles to register their votes. So they tended not to come very often!

The original Romans were pastoralists, and their earliest settlement on the site of Rome was no more than a shepherds' village, as both language (*pecunia* from *pecus* a flock) and legend (Pales, god of shepherds, and Evander, the shepherd-king) can testify. But agriculture proper comes early in the story; the historical records of the Republic are full of edifying stories of legendary farmer-warriors—men like Cincinnatus, who left his plough-oxen in the field, and wiped the muck off his hands before accepting the supreme authority of dictator at a time of crisis (see Ch. I h). The notion that Rome owed her greatness to a sturdy breed of smallholders, content with little above bare subsistence, and working their plots with their own hands, was very well entrenched. Indeed, it survived several major changes in the pattern of land use, including the slave-run plantations of central Italy, and the ranching that came to dominate the south. The peasant economy on which the legends were founded never disappeared, but the strength of the superimposed myths can still be felt in some of the great odes written by the poet Horace as part of the imperial programme of national recovery after the civil wars:

a manly breed of rustic soldiers, taught to turn the sod with Sabine hoes, and to carry out timber from the forest at the bidding of a stern mother, while the sun shifted the shadows on the mountains, and lifted the yoke from the wearied oxen, bringing on the hour of relaxation with his retreating chariot... (Odes III.6.37–44)

This powerful, almost obsessive, morality myth is peculiar to the Romans. In the Greek tradition, from Hesiod's *Works and Days* onwards there are few signs of illusion on the subject.[10] The reason is not hard to discover; in a land where fertile arable soil was rare, and every harvest a hard-won victory obtained by unremitting labour, the myths are firmly centred on the gods who give the victory, on Demeter and Persephone, and Triptolemos, the god of the thrice-ploughed furrow; does not Hesiod himself speak of the process of fallowing not merely as a normal feature, but as man's protection against famine (*Works and Days*, 464)?

The great bulk of our evidence about life in the Greek cities is confined to a single city, Athens, and to a particular period of her history—the late fifth century B.C., as reflected in the surviving comedies of Aristophanes, and in the many fragments from his lost plays and those of his stage rivals.[11] When considering the contrast and the antagonism between town and country, we must take account of the fact that the evidence, though plentiful, is one-sided;

Aristophanes often presents an idealized picture of life on the farm, and exaggerates the wickedness of life in town. But the cleavage between townsmen and country folk cannot be denied, since it was based on important differences in social and economic conditions. Farmers are often presented as victims of the city economy, especially of the play of market forces. The farmer must take his produce to market, but once there he is the victim of sharp practice, and feels that he cannot win! There are deeper divisions between town and country, as old Strepsiades explains to his son in some detail:

> Oh dear! To hell with that marriage-broker who egged me on to marry your poor
> mother. My life in the country was paradise, untidy, easy-going, unrestrained,
> Flowing with honey-bees, sheep and olive-cakes
> But when I married—I, a rustic—her
> A high-stepping city type, niece of the Megacleses,
> A proud, luxurious aristocrat.
> And when I married her, I went to bed
> Smelling of wine-lees, fig-boards, wool-packs,
> She was all perfume, sex, and saffron.   (Aristoph., *Clouds*, 41 ff.)

The peasant who marries the city girl is conscious of a difference of smell: he feels himself inferior in this intimate matter as well as in other aspects. The distinction of manners is already beginning to make itself felt in the language. During the fifth century the word *asteios*—a townsman—is beginning to take on the meaning of 'smart', while *agroikos*—a countryman—goes through a similar process and acquires the meaning 'rude', 'boorish'.

Rather more than a century later, when the philosopher Theophrastus wrote his sketches he included in his portrait-gallery a Boor (*Agroikos*). By now the difference of tone is marked:

> The Boor is the sort of person who will take a purgative before setting out for the
> Assembly, swear that thyme smells just as sweet as perfume, wears shoes too big for
> him, and talks at the top of his voice . . . he is good at sneaking food from the larder
> and eating it, . . . making love on the sly with the bakehouse wench, and then helping
> her grind the corn for the entire establishment, himself included, and so on.[12]
> (*Characters*, I V)

The countryman is no longer merely a figure of fun, but a butt for ridicule. A parallel may be found in more recent times in the growth of the stock image of the country bumpkin, Sir Tunbelly Clumsy, and other clodhopping literary types, which accompanied the elaborate manners and exaggerated posturings of the fop, the dandy and the man-about-town in eighteenth-century England. Certainly one cannot imagine a character like Menander's Surly Old Man (the *Dyskolos*[13] who gives the recently-discovered comedy its title) appearing in the heyday of the fifth century. Aristophanes' *Acharnians*, the nearest neighbours

to *Dyskolos* in surliness, are after all not farmers but charcoal-burners, tradition-
ally a very tough and uncompromising body of men.

The country as a place of escape from the increasing complexities and
inanities of city life seems to be an essentially Roman development, a product,
like the English weekend, of the growth of *Megalopolis*. The citizens of the
average Greek city, whose population was small enough for people to know
each other, and whose extent was no greater than the range of the town-crier's
voice,[14] were so enmeshed in the surrounding countryside that the conditions
favouring an escapist, or weekender's, attitude towards the scene of their day-
to-day activities did not exist. The *cri de coeur* of disconsolate Athenians huddled
together in hastily constructed and makeshift accommodation, longing to see
their vines and orchards, was the exceptional result of a deliberate act of government policy (see Ch. I c).

But what of conditions in much more populous cities such as Alexandria or
Antioch, where populations topped the half-million mark? Did their inhabitants
find adequate means of relaxation within the city limits? Presumably Egypt's
cosmopolitan capital offered less explosive diversions than Jew-baiting by
Greeks and Greek-baiting by Jews?

As for Roman Italy, her towns were for the most part dormitories for those
who farmed within reach of their walls.[15] When Rome regained possession of
the important allied city of Capua after its defection to Hannibal in the Second
Punic War, the ringleaders were punished with the utmost rigour of the law,
but the city itself was allowed to remain unsacked, 'so that the farmers should
have somewhere to live'.[16] Rome, once she had grown to be the capital of the
Italian federation, was a different matter. As life became noisier and the atmosphere more polluted, her wealthy citizens began the process of seasonal
migration that ultimately filled much of the Campanian coastal belt and the
Alban hills with scores of country villas.

The earliest recorded case of a Roman who possessed a country villa of his
own is that of Scipio Africanus, the conqueror of Hannibal. It was at Liternum,
a stern fortress of a place with a very crude bath-house and a farm: Scipio took
his coat off and worked the land himself for profit. The philosopher Seneca,
who visited Liternum, writes:

> I have seen the house ... its cistern hidden by buildings and shrubbery ... and the
> tiny little bath-house, buried in gloom after the fashion of our ancestors. They didn't
> believe in taking a hot bath except in the dark. *Letter* 86 (Ch. IX c)

The wealth that poured into Rome from her succession of eastern conquests
soon led to the superseding of such rudimentary arrangements by leisure establishments designed to meet higher standards of comfort and hygiene, and the
country villa began to play its proper part in Roman society as a place for
relaxation, both physical and mental.[17] Earlier, Scipio's adopted son Aemilianus
and his great friend Laelius are reported to have engaged at their country

retreat in such harmless forms of relaxation as chasing each other round the table, wielding knotted handkerchiefs, while the vegetables were cooking (Horace, *Satires* II.1.71–4).

It was at the beginning of the last century of the Republic that the great exodus to the country began. The general C. Marius (six times consul) led the way and started a fashion, followed by his great rival Sulla. A long time before the dictatorship of Caesar sounded the death-knell of the Republic, the valleys within reach of the capital were dotted with country seats, and along the coast between Cumae and Naples the fashionable seaside villa was developing fast, accompanied by equally fashionable seaside resorts such as Baiae, which, from all accounts, seems to have combined the vulgar attractions of Brighton or Blackpool with the more sophisticated (and more corrupt) activities associated with Biarritz or Monte Carlo.[18] Many Romans of this period had more than one country seat. Cicero, whose grateful clients more than made up for the theoretical disadvantage suffered by Roman barristers (who were not supposed to be paid for their services in the law courts), possessed no fewer than seven of these establishments, as well as a sumptuously decorated town mansion. It was in these surroundings that Romans of the late Republic and early Empire discovered the countryside (seaside as well as inland) as a source of inward enjoyment and aesthetic delight.

It has often been asserted that ancient attitudes differed profoundly from those of modern times in this matter. The great divide here is however not between the ancient world and ours of the twentieth century, but between the pre- and post-romantic eras. If we examine the evidence carefully, we shall find that the Romans of the first Augustan age were not so very different in their outlook on nature from those of the eighteenth-century Augustans.

Both Augustan ages disliked nature in the raw, and wanted her tamed. This was an easier task in ancient Italy than in eighteenth-century England, since man's impact on the landscape had already clothed much of her slopes with olives, vines and orchards; all that now remained was to enjoy the 'amenities'. The words *amoenus* and *amoenitas* were now highly fashionable terms as applied to the sedate pleasures and comforts of country life. Here for example is Cicero, writing to his friend Atticus from his villa on the coast at Formiae: 'You ask me, and you seem to think I don't know, whether I get more pleasure out of hills and scenic prospects than out of a walk along the beach. As you say, both places give me so much pleasure that I simply don't know which is to be preferred (Att. XIV.13.7). For Cicero the ultimate in relaxation was to sit on the shore and count the waves as they came in (Att. II.6.1).

The first townsfolk to invade the countryside were looking for the simple life. This remains the aim right up to the end of the Roman Republic and into the Augustan Age. Simple country pleasures and country fare are the fashion, but of course they are achieved with lots of servants and no chores. The poems of Horace are full of this theme. Thus when his great patron and benefactor visits the poet on the Sabine farm bestowed by him on his protégé, he will not be drinking vintage Falernian, nor even a decent Formian, but *vin ordinaire* or, as the locals now call it, *vino del paese*. 'Cheap local Sabine is all you'll get if you dine with me; if you want vintage stuff, you'll have to wait till you get home' (*Odes* 1.20.1). Augustan man must accept what nature provides. As for man, the creator of comfort, who bends nature to his purposes, there is no place for him in this age of return to plain living and high thinking. Indeed, contemporary poetry is full of sharp criticism of millionaires who extend their seaside porticoes by dumping rubble into the sea, or seek to outdo their neighbours in the height of their columns or the vulgarity of their interior furnishings.[19] But two generations later the vogue is all for deception, for walls decorated with false windows and artificial painted gardens that deceive the eye, and for revolving dining rooms and other technological marvels, where science has created such wonders that the owners of these fabulous villas do not know where nature ends and art begins.

Most of our information on these extravaganzas comes from a bundle of occasional poems called *Silvae* or 'Impromptu Pieces' by the poet Statius, who was born in Naples around A.D. 40. I cannot here do full justice to the technological marvels in which this poet delights; they include a graphic account of the building of a new road (*Silv.* IV.3), the emperor Domitian's new palace (*Silv.* IV.2), and other royal conceits. I shall confine myself to some of the more remarkable passages in the poet's account of two private masterpieces; the villa of Vopiscus at Tivoli (*Silv.* I.3) and that of Pollius Felix at Sorrento (*Silv.* II.2). The chief interest at Tivoli is the lavish plumbing: 'The gilded ceiling beams . . . the patterned veins of glittering marble, the water nymphs that speed their way through every bedroom—shall these move me to wonder?' (I.3.34 ff.); the bath system is so ingeniously contrived that the river, chained to the steaming furnace, laughs at the nymphs that gasp for breath in the stream hard by (ibid. 45–6). Pollius' villa was established in a wilderness of rocks on the famous Sorrento peninsula. But his architects and engineers soon altered the landscape to the owner's tastes: 'Here where you now see level ground, there used to be a hill; the halls you are entering were wild country; where now tall groves appear there was not even any soil; the owner has subdued the place; . . . see how the cliff learns to bear the yoke, how the dwellings force their way in, and the mountain is ordered to withdraw.' A triumph of technology. (*Silv.* II.2.54 ff.)

From these extravagant masterpieces it is time to make our descent to the humbler levels of country life. But where shall we look to make contact with the realities of life in the countryside? It is not easy to find passages in Greek or Roman writers in which we can recognize the genuine sights and sounds and smells—the toil and sweat, the lack of amenities for all except the absentee owner and the friends he takes down with him for a weekend or perhaps a longer holiday (*peregrinatio*), when the Senate is in recess. On a slave-run estate even the supervisory jobs were no sinecures; the manager was first away into the fields at daybreak, and last home at night to prevent stragglers from sneaking off to temporary freedom (Colum. I.8.11). As for peasant farmers—the so-called backbone of the Roman state before the rot set in—their basic supplies had to be brought in the hard, back-breaking way, the water hauled by bucket from the well, the firewood humped on the back from the timber lot, and the goods bought on rare visits to the market brought home, as they still are in Spain and southern Italy, by donkeys with panniers or sacks. There are clear reflections of the harsh realities in Hesiod and Theocritus.[20] Virgil's *Georgics* occasionally give a glimpse of the daily routines of the humble smallholder (1.273-5): 'Often the farmer drives the sluggish donkey, loading its sides with oil or cheap apples, while on the return trip he brings back from town a grooved millstone or a lump of dark pitch.' There is a touch of realism here, but the *Cottar's Saturday Night* atmosphere partially conceals the truth beneath a warm, homely glow: (*Georgics* 1.291-6): 'And there is one who, by the late winter firelight stays awake, splitting wood for torches with a sharp cleaver; meantime his wife, easing the tedium of the task with singing, runs through the warp with tuneful shuttle, or boils down the new wine with fire, skimming off the frothing liquid in the bubbling caldron with leaves.'

One surviving poem of country life, the anonymous 'Country Salad' (*Moretum*) (Ch. I m) sounds the authentic note. The narrative is clear and uncomplicated; the early morning routines and chores are taken directly from the life; and there are no romantic overtones. Nearest in flavour among Virgil's early works is the 'Tavern Entertainer' (*Copa*), followed, at some distance, by the story of the old settler and his productive little plot, inserted into the Fourth *Georgic* (Ch. IX f).

These, however, are only glimpses. To get anywhere near the harsh realities of life as lived by those millions of peasant farmers whose labours made possible the luxurious life-styles of the upper classes of the Roman Empire, one must look to their counterparts in the world of today. In the overcrowded flood-plains of Bangladesh, and the overworked, eroded flats of Bihar the margin between subsistence and starvation is perilously narrow. Here the current realities help to fill out the meagre, often laconic, ancient references to competition between humans and animals for food, and to local famines, when the population has been reduced to eating grass and vetch (Ch. I l). But there is one important difference between their world and ours. Modern communications mean that supplies of grain, of dried milk, of medicines, together with teams of doctors and nurses, can be flown in to give immediate aid to stricken communities. In antiquity, on the contrary, the margin between survival and starvation was narrow, and there were no rapid communications.

We should not fool ourselves into thinking that the elaborate network of Roman roads as shown on the maps provided the means of escape from starvation: 'We shall never understand the life of the towns of the Greco-Roman world unless we relive through the texts, the creeping fear of famine . . . Each small town knew that they would have to face out alone a winter of starvation, if ever their harvest failed.'[21] The stark reality can be detected here and there in the agronomists: to get the full impact we need to travel with Apollonius through the market at Aspendos in Asia (Ch. I l) where there was only vetch for sale and the inhabitants were eating this and anything else they could lay their hands on.[22]

The critical reader may well complain that many of the 'expected questions' suggested earlier (above, p. 1) have not been answered. Some of those that relate to the manners and customs of the countryside are answered in the body of the text (see especially Chapters VIII and IX), others in the accompanying illustrations, which are not a mere bonus, but essential to the book. Of the remainder, the most intractable by far are questions concerning status and social relations. Some country folk have proved to be rather less inarticulate than Rostovtzeff supposed (above, p. 1): but what of the ubiquitous slaves? What effect did they have on country life? What culture did they have? We do not know. The inscriptions on their tombstones speak of long service and devotion to their masters; but these stereotypes are just as uninformative as those illuminated addresses presented to retiring veterans by company directors nowadays. And what about social mobility in the countryside? City slaves could pocket their perks, accumulate a *peculium*, and gain their freedom either that way or through the deathbed generosity of their owners; some freed slaves and sons of slaves made fortunes and achieved great political influence; others (and there were plenty in this category) had unspectacular careers, but made a modest competence. It would appear that farm slaves had nothing to look forward to save the charity of their owners when they were too old for the heavy manual labour of the farm. Did most owners follow Cato's advice (*On Agriculture* 11.7) to treat old slaves like old oxen and worn-out implements, and sell them? And what prospects were there for the peasant farmer, and for the men who sold their labour at harvest or vintage time? Is the case of the Maktar reaper (Ch. VII n) to be regarded as unique, or were there perhaps others who both shared his attitude and succeeded in rising above his class?[23] Most free men who worked on the land in his day were tenants on private or imperial estates, and between patron and dependant a great gulf was fixed. The material gap was evident enough, as Professor MacMullen reminds us: 'On the two sides of the gate, two worlds: one with a dirt floor, one with a mosaic.'[24]

The Greek city-states spent much of their time fighting one another; their futile disputes over boundaries continued long after they had lost their independence to Rome; but from an early stage foreigners who could not speak Greek (*barbaroi*) came to be regarded as inferior. Native Romans, on the other hand, while they took pride in the Latin language, and in their distinctive formal dress (the *toga*), did not reach such depths of racialism.

Once away from his homeland in Greece or Italy, the Greek or Roman found himself among 'people divided from us by language' (as John Chrysostom calls them), conquered by his forefathers and subjected to another civilization without easily becoming a part of it. In cities and in the pieces of cities broken off—rich rural villas—he would be understood. Once outside, however, a thickening accent gradually gave way, mile by mile, to a total ignorance of the master tongues. In their stead, Aramaic, Phrygian, Arabic, Punic, Berber, Thracian.[25]

The relationship between townspeople and country folk was thus a complicated one, not to be assessed in terms of any neat formula. When conditions on the land deteriorated, and hungry peasants migrated to the city, they were treated by the authorities as brutally as if they were Jews or other vulnerable aliens, the victims of periodic expulsion orders.[26] Yet the relationship was a symbiotic one, with needs to be met on either side, however great the inequalities, however evident the exploitation of the peasantry by the landowners who drew their profits from the endless labours in the fields.

No monument serves better to dramatize this relationship than the amphitheater at El-Djem, in southern Tunisia; nothing prepares the traveller for its revelation. Set back behind a scattering of a few twisting streets of one- or two-story whitewashed houses in an altogether unimpressive little town, it soars a hundred feet and more into the air. Sixty thousand spectators could be seated in it. What paid for it, in a land now semi-desert? The answer, oil. For miles around, in Roman times, grew vast olive orchards, with cereal crops in furrows between the rows of trees, requiring the labor of a population of tenant farmers and laborers ten times what the region would support today. Landlords, their names now unknown, grew rich from the yield and built the amphitheater as a gift for a town in which the citizens—men, women and children—nowhere near sufficed to fill the seats ... the seats were filled, however,—by the countryfolk streaming in on festival days to stare, laugh, clap and shriek at vastly expensive shows put on for free by the very landlords that exploited their labors in the sun.[27]

This passage comes at the conclusion of Ramsay MacMullen's notable discussion of rural-urban relations in the Roman world. This and many other aspects of the subject are illustrated in the following pages, in which the countryside is allowed to speak for itself.

1. M. I. Rostovtzeff, *Social and Economic History of the Roman Empire*, p.192. Much light is thrown on many aspects of country life in the illustrations to this work, described by the author as 'an essential part of the book' (p.xvii).

2. See Pausanias, *Tour of Greece*, x.4.1 for a list of the essential features of a Greek city.

3. See e.g. Ch. I e, *The boor*; cf. Terence, *The Brothers*, where the attitudes of country-bred Demea and his city-bred brother Micio are sharply contrasted.

4. See Ch. VII l; cf. *Letters*, III.19.6; VII.30.2–3; VIII.2.15.1.

5. See Ch. I n; a petition from tenants of an imperial estate near Carthage, complaining of illegal exactions.

6. See Ch. IV e.

7. A similar air of contempt pervades Juvenal's Fifteenth Satire.

8. V. Ehrenberg, *The People of Aristophanes*, p.84 (in a chapter containing many helpful references on this topic).

9. 'The true city in classical antiquity encompassed both the *chora*, the rural hinterland, and an urban centre, where . . . the community had its administration and its public cults' (M. I. Finley, *The Ancient Economy*, p.123).

10. An obvious exception is, of course, Theocritus: 'In Theokritos's own lifetime Sicily and South Italy were repeatedly devastated and impoverished by war and pillage; yet his herdsmen never betray any awareness that their animals are in danger of being slaughtered by hungry mercenaries' (K. J. Dover, *Theocritus: Select Poems*, p.lvi). On the other hand, the harvesters of Idyll X (Ch. IX b) are not conventional pastoral swains, but working men.

11. Discussed in detail, with copious references, by Ehrenberg, p.73 ff.

12. See the full text (Ch. I e).

13. See Ch. III b.

14. See Aristotle, *Politics*, I.1326b.6 f.

15. See my *Roman Farming*, p.50, and references cited there.

16. Livy, 26.16.7 (see further *Roman Farming, loc. cit.* n.15).

17. See e.g. Cicero, *On Oratory*, II.22: 'the true way to enjoy leisure is not to strain the mind, but to relax the strain'; on changing attitudes towards work and leisure see J.-M. André, *Recherches sure l'Otium romain* and *L'Otium dans la vie morale et intellectuelle romaine*.

18. See J. H. d'Arms, *Romans on the Bay of Naples*.

19. See Horace, *Odes* III.1.33 ff.; II.18.20–2; III.24.3–4 (Building out over the sea); ibid. (Interior splendour).

20. Hesiod: Ch. IV e; Theocritus: Ch. IX b; cf. Calpurnius Siculus, *Eclogues* III.1 ff.

21. Peter Brown, *Roman Society in the Age of St Augustine*, p.15; cf. MacMullen, *Roman Social Relations*, ch. 11.

22. Ch. I l; MacMullen (*RSR*, p.158, n.18) considers the historicity of this incident doubtful, but adds: 'but perhaps . . . if it is fiction, its claim to typicality is strengthened.'

23. MacMullen (*RSR*, p.47) cites a handful of parallel cases, adding that 'indirect evidence suggests quite a widespread phenomenon'.

24. MacMullen (*RSR*, p.45).

25. MacMullen (*RSR*, p.45 f.).

26. See Lewis and Reinhold, *Roman Civilization*, p.438 ff. An edict of A.D. 215, expelling from the capital of Egypt 'all Egyptians and particularly the country folk who have fled from other parts and can easily be detected . . .'

27. MacMullen (*RSR*, pp.55–6).

I(a) Similes from nature sharpen the picture of strife

Homer, *Iliad* III.1–37

Now when all were drawn up in order, each tribe under its commander, the Trojans came on with noise and clamour like the clamour of cranes that rises up before the face of heaven as they flee before winter and the copious rains;

13

with clamour they fly towards Ocean's streams, bringing death and destruction to the Pygmies, and launch their murderous assault at daybreak. But the Achaeans came on in silence, breathing valour, resolved in their hearts to defend each other. Like the mist that the South Wind spreads about the mountain peaks, no friend to shepherds, but better than the night to thieves, when a man can see no further than a stone's throw; so rose up from their advancing ranks a cloud of dust, and swiftly they marched across the plain . . .

When valiant Menelaus saw Paris advancing towards him in front of the host with long strides, he was happy as a hungry lion when he has lighted on the carcass of an antlered stag or a wild goat, and devours it greedily despite the efforts of the swift hounds and doughty hunters to drive him off, so Menelaus rejoiced when he espied godlike Paris: for he thought that he should have his revenge on the man who wronged him. At once he leapt down from his chariot to the ground fully armed. When godlike Paris saw him appearing in the fore-front, his heart utterly failed him, and he slunk back among his men, avoiding death, like a man who sees a snake in a mountain glen, and starts back; trembling seizes his limbs beneath him, and he retreats the way he came, and pallor fills his cheeks. Thus godlike Paris slunk back among the lordly Trojans, in terror of the son of Atreus.

I(b) The two kinds of strife

Hesiod, *Works and Days* 8–43

There was never really only one kind of strife. There are two kinds on earth. As for the one, a man would like her when he got to know her; but the other one is culpable. They are utterly different in nature. The one fosters evil wars and battle, cruel as she is; nobody loves her, but under compulsion, and through this will of the immortals men pay honour to this oppressive strife. But the other one was born the elder daughter of dark Night, and the son of Kronos, who sits on high and dwells in the bright air, set her in the roots of the earth; and she is far more kind to men. She rouses even the shiftless man to toil; a man grows eager to work when he looks at his rich neighbour, who presses on with his ploughing and planting, and the good ordering of his house. So neighbour competes with his neighbour who presses on in search of wealth. This strife is a good friend to mortals. Then potter is angry with potter, and craftsman with craftsman; beggar is jealous of beggar, and singer of singer.

Perses, lay up these things firmly in your heart, and do not let that strife who delights in mischief keep you from your work as you peep and eavesdrop on the wrangles of the meeting place. He has little time for quarrels and lawsuits who hasn't a whole year's sustenance stacked away within, the produce of the earth, Demeter's grain.

I(c) A mass evacuation from country to town

Thucydides II.14–16

The Athenians listened to Pericles' advice, and started to bring in their wives and children from the country, together with all their household effects, even down to the woodwork of their houses, which they dismantled. Their sheep and cattle they sent over to Euboea and the adjacent islands. But the evacuation was a difficult operation, since the majority of them had always been used to living in the countryside . . . Even after the unification of Attica under Theseus, old habits still prevailed, and from early times down to the present conflict most Athenians have lived in the country with their families and households, and were consequently far from happy at being uprooted, especially as they had only recently restored their establishments after the Persian invasion . . . So it was with deep sadness and reluctance that they now abandoned their homes and the venerable shrines of their ancient community, and prepared to alter their whole way of life, leaving behind what each man regarded as his native city.

I(d) The rustic hero and the delights of peace

Aristophanes, *Peace* 1127–1206

CHORUS: Oh! Joy, Joy! No more helmet, cheese or onions! I have no lust for fighting; what I love is to go on drinking with good comrades in the ingle by the fire when good dry wood, uprooted in the height of summer, is crackling; to cook pease on the coals, and beechnuts in the embers, to kiss my pretty Thracian slave while my wife is in the bath. Nothing is nicer, when the god is sprinkling our crops with gentle showers, than to natter with a neighbour, saying, 'Tell me Komarchides, what'll we do today? I'd love to drink my fill, while the god is doing us good.' Come, wife, roast me three measures of beans, mix in with them some flour, and pick out some figs. Syra! Call in Manes from the fields; it's out of the question to prune the vines today or dig round them while the ground is damp. Let someone bring me the thrush and that pair of chaffinches; there was some beestings in the house and four pieces of hare, unless the cat stole some of them last evening; at any rate there was a clatter and a right big uproar in the house. Serve me up three portions, boy, and give my dad the fourth. Go and ask Aeschinades for some myrtle branches with the berries on; and then—it's on the same road—go call Charinades over to drink with me to the health of the god who blesses and increases our crops.

When the grasshopper sings his sweet song I love to take a look around and see if the Lemnian vines are ripening yet (they are the early-ripening ones), and to watch the figs filling out, and when they are ripe I eat them with gusto, and cry out 'What a glorious season!' Then I bruise some thyme and mix a julep. Then I get fat at this time in the summer, instead of watching a blasted captain with his triple plume and his cloak of startling crimson (he calls it Sardian purple!); whenever he has to fight a battle in it, he dyes himself with Cyzicene saffron; then he's first to run away, shaking his plumes like some great yellow prancing cock, while I'm left behind to watch the nets. When they're back home, they behave abominably. Some of us they put on the muster list, others they scratch out, and that two or three times over. Tomorrow's the day for going to the front, and one poor wretch has brought no rations, because he didn't know he was down to serve; he halts in front of the statue of Pandion, sees his name there, is dumbfounded, and starts running, with an acid look.

This is how they treat us rustics, those who only know how to throw their shields away. The townsfolk they treat less scurvily. For this I'll still call the rascals to account, god willing. They've certainly done me a lot of harm; they are lions in peacetime, but foxes when it comes to the fighting.

TRYGAEUS: My, my! What a crowd for the wedding feast! Hey, dust the tables with this here crest: it's good for nothing else now. Then bring out the cakes, the thrushes, plenty of good jugged hare, and the baps.

SICKLE-MAKER: Trygaeus, where's Trygaeus?

TR: I'm boiling thrushes.

SM: Trygaeus, my best of friends, what a fine stroke of business, a very good turn you've done me by making Peace! Before this I couldn't have got anyone to pay me even an obol apiece for my sickles, but now I'm selling them at fifty drachmas! This chap here is getting three drachmas apiece for wine-casks for the farm. Come then, Trygaeus, take as many sickles and casks as you like for nothing. And please accept them; it's out of our handsome profits on the sales that we're offering you these wedding presents.

I(e) The boor

Theophrastus, *Characters* IV

Boorishness would seem to be an unseemly ignorance, and the boor to be the sort of person who will take a purgative before he goes to the Assembly, declare that thyme smells just as sweet as perfume, wear shoes too big for his feet, and talk at the top of his voice. Distrusting his friends and kinsfolk he

confides matters of great importance to his servants, and gives a full account of
what went on at the Assembly to the hired hands on his farm.

He will sit down with his cloak hitched above his knees, exposing his private
parts. He is neither surprised nor frightened by anything he sees on the street,
but let him catch sight of an ox or a donkey or a billy-goat, and he will stand
and gaze at it. He is good at sneaking food from the larder and eating it, and
drinking his wine too strong, and making love on the sly with the bakehouse
wench, and then helping her grind the corn for the whole establishment, himself included. He likes to give the beasts their provender while munching his
breakfast, and to answer the door himself . . . he is also addicted to singing in
the baths, and loves to drive hobnails into his shoes.

I(f) A boor of a poet

Catullus XXII

Dear Varus—your most proper friend Suffenus
is a charming person, witty and urbane.
Besides, his verse production is a record—
ten thousand lines, I calculate (or more)
he's written out—and not on palimpsest
like most of us—no, paper royal, new books,
new bosses, scarlet thongs and vellum covers,
the whole lead-ruled and levelled off with pumice.
But, when you read them, that nice urban man
Suffenus seems the merest clodhopper
or digger—he's so different, so absurd.
What shall we put it down to? Quondam wit
(or something even wittier than that)
becomes more boring than the boring country
as soon as he touches poetry. And yet
he's never happier than when writing 'pomes',
so self-congratulant, so self-admiring.
We all, I fancy, have that fault—there's no one
who's not, you'll find, *suffenous* in some way.
Each one of us is stuck with his illusion,
but we can't see the sack we're carrying.

GUY LEE

I(g) Trouble on Regulus' farm

Valerius Maximus IV.4.6

Atilius Regulus, a namesake and relative of this man, whose name is linked with the greatest success and the worst disaster of the First Punic War, after smashing the proud might of Carthage in Africa with a series of victories, was informed that his successful conduct of operations had led to the extension of his command for a further year. He then wrote to the senate, telling them that the manager of his little four-acre farm in the Pupinian district had died, and that a hired farm hand had seized his opportunity to decamp with the entire stock and equipment; he therefore begged them to send out a replacement, to prevent his wife and children from starving. When the consul communicated his despatch to the senators, orders were given to have the farm leased, to supply provisions for his wife and children, and to replace his lost equipment at public expense. So highly esteemed was the valour of Atilius, on which Rome will pride herself for all time to come.

I(h) Cincinnatus

Dionysius of Halicarnassus, *Roman Antiquities* x.8.4-5

To pay off the costs incurred in rebutting the charges against his son, Cincinnatus sold up most of his properties, leaving nothing for himself except for one little holding on the far side of the Tiber, on which there was a humble cottage; and there, cultivating the farm with the help of a few slaves, he led a hard-working and humdrum life; because of his sorrow and his poverty he neither visited the city nor went to greet his friends, nor took part in the festivals, nor allowed himself any other kind of diversion.

Meanwhile the senate sent men to invite the consul and escort him to Rome to take up his office. It happened that Quinctius was at that moment ploughing a piece of ground for sowing, and he was himself following the gaunt oxen that were breaking the fallow. He had no tunic on, and was wearing a small loincloth and a cap. On seeing a crowd of people coming on to the field he halted his plough, and was for some time at a loss to know who they were, and what business had brought them there. Then, when someone ran up to him and told him to make himself more presentable, he went into the cottage, put on some clothes, and re-emerged. At this the men sent to escort him all greeted him, not by name, but officially as consul and, attiring him in his official robes, and placing in front of him the axes and other official insignia, they invited him to follow them to the city. And he, pausing for a moment and shedding tears, said only this: 'So my field will not be sown this year, and we shall be in danger of not having the wherewithal to live.'

I(j) A bad political gaffe
Valerius Maximus VII.5.2

P. Scipio Nasica was a bright star in the political firmament; as consul he declared war against Jugurtha; in his pure, unsoiled hands he received the image of the Great Mother of Ida, when she migrated from her home in Phrygia to our altars and homes; he suppressed many dangerous revolutionary outbreaks by the force of his personal prestige, when the senate for several years was proud to own him as its leading light. As a young man standing for the office of Curule Aedile, he happened, in the usual run of canvassing, to grasp rather firmly a citizen's hand, which had been roughened by farm labour. In jesting mood he asked the man whether he was in the habit of walking on his hands. The remark was picked up by bystanders, and passed on to the public at large; and this was the reason for Scipio's failure to secure election; all the rustic tribes, taking the remark as an insulting reflection on their poverty, made his offensive witticism a focus for their wrath.

I(k) The decline in farming standards
Columella, *On Farming* I.Preface.13–18

There remains, as I have said, one way of increasing one's fortune that is upright and above board, and this comes from cultivating the soil. If the principles of this science were put into practice as they were in earlier days, even haphazardly, by people without knowledge (provided they were the owners of the land), husbandry would be suffering less damage: the effort that goes with ownership would largely make up for the losses resulting from lack of knowledge; and men who had their own interests at stake would not wish throughout their lives to be conspicuously ignorant of their own business; being for that reason more anxious to learn, they would get a thorough grounding in husbandry. As it is, we not only think it beneath our dignity to work our estates with our own hands, but we do not think it at all important to appoint as manager the most experienced man we have, or at least, in default of experience, one who is active and wide-awake, so that he can quickly learn what he doesn't know. But if a rich man buys a farm, he selects from his crowd of footmen and litter-bearers the most enfeebled in years and vigour, and sends him off to the farm, disregarding the fact that this particular job demands not only knowledge, but the liveliness of a man in his prime, allied to bodily strength, to cope with its hardships. Or, if the owner is a man of modest fortune, he takes someone from among his hired hands, who now refuses him the daily monetary payment, and orders him to be made foreman, when he has no knowledge of the task he is to supervise.

When I take note of this, frequently pondering and reflecting on the shameful consensus with which rural discipline has been abandoned and become a thing of the past, my fear is that men of free birth may regard it as base and in some way degrading or dishonourable. But when I am reminded by the great number of written records that our ancestors regarded attention to farming as a matter of pride; from this came Quinctius Cincinnatus, summoned from the plough to the dictatorship to rescue a beleaguered consul and his army; and then, laying down the power which he handed back after victory more speedily than he had assumed it for command, returned once more to the same bullocks, and his little ancestral inheritance of four *iugera*.* From farming came also Gaius Fabricius and Curius Dentatus, the former after expelling Pyrrhus from Italy, the latter after subduing the Sabines, tilling their seven *iugera* of captured territory, which they had received in individual distributions, with an energy equal to the bravery they had displayed in gaining it. I shall avoid an inopportune discussion of individual cases at this time, when I observe that so many outstanding leaders of Roman birth were invariably distinguished for this combined occupation of defending and cultivating their inherited or acquired estates. I realize that the manners and strenuous lifestyle of bygone days are out of favour with present-day extravagance and voluptuous living. Just as Marcus Varro complained in the days of our grandfathers, all of us who are heads of families have abandoned the sickle and the plough, and slunk inside the city, using our hands in the circus and the theatre instead of in the cornfields and vineyards . . . But by Hercules, that true stock of Romulus, getting as much exercise from working in the fields as from continual hunting, possessed outstanding physical strength and, toughened by the labours of peace, easily endured the rigours of war when occasion demanded, and always thought more highly of common country folk than of townees. Those who dawdled about within the precincts of the country houses were regarded as lazier than those who worked the land outside; in the same way, those who loafed inside the walls in the shelter of the city were thought to be more indolent than those who tilled the soil or supervised the labours of the tillers . . .

I(1) A famine relieved

Philostratus, *Life of Apollonius of Tyana* 1.15

When he came to Aspendos in Pamphylia . . . he found nothing for sale in the market except vetches, and the citizens were feeding on these and anything else

---

iugerum two-thirds of an acre.

they could get; for the rich men had stored away all the grain, and were holding it for export. As a result, an excited crowd of all ages had assaulted the Mayor, and were lighting a fire with the intention of burning him alive, although he was clutching the statues of the emperor . . . Apollonius turned to the bystanders, and gestured to them that they should listen; they were astonished, and not only held their tongues, but placed their fire on the altars that were at hand. At this the Mayor plucked up courage and said 'So-and-so and So-and-so,' naming several people, 'are responsible for the famine: they have removed the grain and are holding it in several parts of the country.' A hue and cry then went up among the Aspendians, who wanted to rush off to the estates of these people, but Apollonius shook his head to tell them not to do that, but instead to summon the culprits and get the grain from them with their consent. When they arrived, he very nearly broke into speech against them, he was so moved by the tears of the crowd . . . but he kept to his vow of silence, and wrote his indictment on a board, and passed it over to the Mayor to be read aloud; the indictment was as follows: 'Apollonius to the grain dealers of Aspendos. The earth is the mother of us all for she is just, but you, because you are unjust, have made her the mother of yourselves alone, and if you do not stop I will not allow you to remain on her.' They were so alarmed by the statement that they swamped the market-place with grain and the city recovered.

I(m) Morning on an Italian smallholding

Anonymous, *The Country Salad* (*Moretum*)

Already night had completed ten of winter's hours, and with his crowing the sentinel bird had proclaimed the coming of day, when Simylus, rustic cultivator of a meagre plot, fearful of bitter hunger on the morrow's morn, slowly, from the cheap pallet where he lay outstretched, raises his limbs, and with anxious hand gropes through the lifeless darkness, feeling for the hearth, and finds it at last, to his hurt. From a burnt-out log there still lingered a tiny whiff of smoke, while the ashes concealed the glow of the embers beneath. With head bent forward he brings his lamp up to them, tilting it forward, draws out with a needle the dried-up wick, and with many a puff, awakes the sluggish fire. At length, after much effort, the hearth takes fire, and he withdraws; with screening hand he protects the light from the draught, and with peering key, opens the closet door. Here on the ground was spread a wretched heap of corn; from this he helps himself to as much as his measure, which runs up to sixteen pounds weight, can take.

And now, moving off, he takes his stand at the mill, and on a tiny shelf, fixed firmly for the purpose to the wall, he sets his trusty light. Then he slips both arms out of his tunic and, dressed in a shaggy goatskin, he carefully sweeps clean the stones and bosom of the mill with a tail. Next he summons his two hands to the work, dividing them between the dual task; the left is bent on feeding in the grain, the right on driving the mill. This, on its endless circuit, turns the mill at speed—the grain, pounded by the stones' swift blows, trickles down; the left hand from time to time supports her wearied sister and takes her turn. At times he sings rustic ditties, and solaces his labours with country songs; at times he shouts for Scybale. She was his helper, of African birth, her whole shape proclaiming her origin. Her hair was twisted, her lips swollen, her colour dark brown, her chest broad, her breasts pendulous, her belly something pinched, her legs thin, her feet broad and ample. Her rough shoes were split and torn in many places. He calls her, and bids her place on the fire some wood for burning, and heat cold water over the flame.

I(n) Excessive demands made upon imperial tenants

Corpus of Latin Inscriptions VIII.10570

. . . that you may be informed about the collusion practised by your imperial agent, not only in conjunction with our enemy Allius Maximus, but with almost all the tenants-in-chief, contrary to justice, and to the ruin of your finances, and beyond the bounds of moderation. The result is that he has, over many years, refrained from investigating our urgent petitions and appeals to your divine rescript. Furthermore, he has encouraged the machinations of the said Allius Maximus, tenant-in-chief, who stands in great favour with him, to such an extent that he has despatched troops to the *saltus Burunitanus*, and given orders for some of us to be roughed up, others fettered, and some, even though they are Roman citizens, to be flogged with rods and cudgels. The sole reason advanced for this treatment was that we had written an outspoken letter, imploring your Majesty's aid, since we find ourselves suffering ill-treatment so severe and so blatant in proportion to our weakness, and this has forced us wretched men to look once again to your divine foresight for aid. We therefore entreat you, most revered emperor, to come to our assistance . . . that the conditions remain as set out in the commentaries of the imperial agents that are deposited in your archive of the *tractus Karthaginiensis*, that we owe not more than two days' labour per year of ploughing, two of hoeing, two of harvesting, and that there may be no dispute, inasmuch as it has been laid down in the general rescript inscribed on bronze, and recognized by all our neighbours on all sides, and confirmed by the commentaries of the imperial agents. Come to our aid; and since we, humble country folk, making a living by the labours of our hands, are unable to stand up to the tenant-in-chief who has gained great favour by his briberies, have pity on us, and by your sacred rescript do not see fit to require us to give more than is due from us in terms of the *Lex Hadriana*, and the letter from your agents, namely, six days' work per year, so that through your Majesty's favour we, the nurslings and little home-born servants of your estates, may suffer no further harassment at the hands of the tenants-in-chief of the fiscal territories.

Reply:

The Emperor Caesar Marcus Aurelius Commodus Antoninus Augustus Sarmatianus Germanicus Maximus to Lucius Lucullus and others whom it may concern; in view of the law and of my decision, tenants-in-chief shall not require more than thrice two days' labour, lest any unjust exaction be made by you in violation of the general rescript. (*in another hand*) I have written; I have certified (*the signature*).

II

LANDSCAPES,
REAL OR IMAGINED

Country people, born and bred, whether ancient or modern, tend to take their surroundings, natural or man-made, for granted. Copses, meadows, olive groves, orchards and vineyards are accepted, sometimes grudgingly approved, along with the natural beauty of the environment, but seldom enthused over; articulate responses of pleasure usually come from outsiders—either visitors from the city, or exiles in foreign lands. The siting of country houses, and especially of temples and shrines, as L. P. Wilkinson reminds us (*The Roman Experience*, 1975), gives the lie to the once fashionable notion that Greeks and Romans had no genuine feeling for landscape. An important distinction is to be noticed, however, between ancient and modern attitudes: a glance at the contents of this chapter will show clearly that the man-made landscape predominates over the wilderness, as indeed it was to continue to predominate for many centuries after the end of the ancient world.

The primeval forests, where they still survived, were, like their medieval counterparts, regarded as the abodes of spirits of the wilderness, personified as Artemis/Diana, mistress of wild animals, or as Pan, the goat-foot god, lord of the high mountains and remote glens of Arcadia. But the haunts of Pan and his nymphs were not densely forested, unlike the frontier country that lay between Rome and her northern neighbours in central Etruria. Livy's account (ix.36.1) of the first expedition into central Etruria reflects the typical reactions of plainsmen on first encountering densely wooded country: 'In those days the Ciminian forest was more impassable and terrifying than were recently the wooded ravines of Germany, and no one—not even a trader—had ever visited it up to that time.' The Romans, whose ancestors had cut down the bush and drained the marshes of their homeland, liked their landscapes tamed. Some of their worst military defeats had occurred in treacherous mountain passes such as the notorious Caudine Forks, or in the dark recesses of the Teutoburger Wald, where three entire legions had come to a miserable end (Tacitus, *Annals*, 1.60 ff). Germanicus' visit to the scene of the catastrophe nearly ended in another disaster on ground 'familiar to the conquerors, but fatal to those who were unfamiliar with the conditions' (Ibid. 63).

Descriptions of landscape can be found in literature as far back as Homer; in the *Iliad* they are excluded from the action, finding a place either in the similes that briefly draw the attention away from the tensions and violence of the narra-

24

tive (see Ch. I a), or in the elaborate imagery of the shield wrought by Hephaistos for Achilles (Ch. II a). Here we are presented with a miracle of landscape, executed in a variety of metals with consummate skill by the god of metal-working himself, the various scenes being inlaid like the dagger-blades found by Schliemann at Mycenae. But the treatment of scenes is fanciful, in tune with the whole account, which begins with a pair of intelligent, supernatural bellows, puffing away industriously at the bidding of the god. In keeping with this flight of fancy is the golden cornfield, which 'grew black behind the ploughmen, just like a real field . . . a miracle of craftsmanship'. The idealized landscape, on the other hand, makes its first appearance in European literature in the *Odyssey*. The vines and fruit-trees in Alkinoos' garden bear fruit all the year round, and the wind blows unendingly from the west (Ch. II b). But the setting is reasonably close to that of everyday life. Calypso's bower, however (*Odyssey* v.59–74), is unmistakably romantic, and its elegantly channelled crystal streams lead forward to the Paradise Gardens of the medieval world (see Pearsall and Salter, *Landscapes and Seasons of the Medieval World*, 1973).

With the *Homeric Hymn to Pan* (Ch. II c) we are transported into an artificial, enchanted landscape, filled, not with the well-ordered activities of a man-made garden, but with the wild abandon of the lord of the untamed wilderness of crag and glen, and of his attendants 'moving with nimble feet, and singing beside some well of dark water, while Echo laments around the mountain top'.

Theocritus' *Seventh Idyll* (Ch. II d) is both an individual masterpiece and an archetype of the genre we call 'pastoral', which later poets were to take up and ultimately to reduce to a stale literary convention. All the 'standard' features of the idyllic landscape are present—shaded waters, abundance of ripe fruit, and the air filled with the singing of birds. The water is sacred, for it flows out of a cave of the nymphs, and the wine that quenches the thirst of the poet and his companions has been mixed by their hands. The whole poem glows with the radiant splendour of a southern landscape (see Ch. VIII c).

The remainder of the chapter is largely taken up with the man-made land-scapes of Italy, observed with care by Lucretius (Ch. II e), or translated into a visionary praise song by Virgil (Ch. II g). From Virgil too comes the elaborate topography of Aeneas' African landfall (Ch. II h), perhaps inspired by a painting, followed by Pliny's splendid description of the landscape around his Tuscan country house, the view of which would cause his guest to suppose that what lay before him 'was not a real, but some painted landscape of surpassing beauty'. Descriptions of what might catch the eye of the traveller on the road are rare. (Horace's *Journey to Brindisi* is unfortunately too long to be included unabridged, and will not stand surgery.) Ch. II k is slight, but gives a few roadside impres-sions, and Namatianus' voyage has been included for the occasional glimpses it gives of coastal features as seen from close inshore (Ch. II n). In spite of the tedious sermonizing on character in relation to climate, Cassiodorus' description of Squillace and its surroundings (Ch. II m) provides a rare example of an ancient writer communicating to the reader his enthusiasm for a landscape known and appreciated for its own sake.

II(a) Scenes on the shield of Achilles

Homer, *Iliad* XVIII.541–606

And in the shield he set a broad field of soft, rich fallow, which was ploughed three times. And in it many ploughmen were driving and turning their yokes of oxen to and fro. And when they reached the headland of the field and made their turn, a man would go the rounds and hand them a cup of honey-sweet wine. Then they turned back along the furrow, eager to reach the headland of the deep fallow. The field, though made of gold, grew black behind them, just like a real field when being ploughed, a miracle of craftsmanship.

Next he set in it a royal estate, where harvesters were working with sharp sickles in their hands. Armfuls of corn fell to the ground in rows along the furrow, while others were being tied up by the binders with wisps of straw. Three of these stood close up, and the lads who were gleaning at their backs kept up a constant supply, bringing up the bundles in their arms. And among them was the king, standing, sceptre in hand, beside the swathe, quietly rejoicing in his heart. In the background, under an oak-tree, the heralds were preparing a feast, cooking a great ox they had slaughtered, and the women were sprinkling the meat for the harvesters' supper with lashings of white barley-meal.

Next he inserted a vineyard heavily laden with clusters of grapes. It was beautifully fashioned in gold, but the clusters were black, and the vineyard was set up throughout with silver props. All round it he ran a trench of blue enamel, and outside that a fence of tin. Only a single pathway led to it, used by the pickers whenever they gathered the vintage. And light-hearted lasses and lads were bringing away the honey-sweet fruit in baskets. And in their midst was a boy playing sweet music on his loud-sounding lyre, and singing with delicate tone the lovely song of Linus. They all beat time with him, and followed the music and the words with dancing feet.

He also set in it a herd of straight-horned cattle; the cows he made of gold and tin. They were mooing as they came hurrying by to the pasture, beside a murmuring stream with its swaying reeds. Four golden herdsmen walked beside the cattle, and nine swift-footed dogs were following them. But up among the leading cows a pair of savage lions had taken a bellowing bull, who roared loudly as they dragged him off. Dogs and young herdsmen came up to the rescue. But the lions, having torn the great bull's hide, were lapping up his dark blood and entrails; to no effect did the herdsmen rouse and egg on their fast hounds, but as for biting, the dogs kept just out of the lions' reach. They stood close by, and barked.

II(b) The gardens of Alkinoos

Homer, *Odyssey* VII.112–32

Outside the courtyard but stretching close up to the gates, and with a hedge running down either side, lies a large orchard of four acres, where trees hang their greenery on high, the pear and the pomegranate, the apple with its glossy burden, the sweet fig and the luxuriant olive. Their fruit never fails nor runs short, winter and summer alike. It comes at all seasons of the year, and there is never a time when the West Wind's breath is not assisting, here the bud and here the ripening fruit; so that pear after pear, apple after apple, cluster on cluster of grapes, and fig upon fig are always coming to perfection. In the same enclosure there is a fruitful vineyard, in one part of which is a warm patch of level ground, where some of the grapes are drying in the sun, while others are gathered or being trodden, and on the foremost rows hang unripe bunches that have just cast their blossom or show the first faint tinge of purple. Vegetable beds of various kinds are neatly laid out beyond the furthest row and make a smiling patch of never-failing green. The garden is served by two springs, one led in rills to all parts of the enclosure, while its fellow opposite, after providing a watering place for the townsfolk, runs under the courtyard gate towards the great house itself. Such were the beauties with which the gods had adorned Alkinoos' home.

E. V. RIEU
(Homer, *The Odyssey*, trans. E. V. Rieu,
Harmondsworth and New York, 1945)

II(c) An enchanted landscape

Homeric Hymn to Pan

Tell me, Muse, about Pan, the dear son of Hermes, the goat-footed and two-horned god, the lover of noise. Through wooded glades he wanders with dancing nymphs who tread the sheer cliff's edge, calling on Pan, the shepherd god, the fine-haired, unwashed one. He has for his domain every snowy ridge, and the mountain peaks, and the craggy summits. Hither and thither he strays through the dense thickets, and, lured on by gentle streams, now he presses on among the towering crags, climbing up to the highest peak that overlooks the flock; often he races through the glistening high mountain ranges, and often he speeds along the shoulders, killing wild beasts, this sharp-eyed god. Only at nightfall, as he returns from the chase, he sounds his call, playing a sweet tune to the pipes; not even *she* could surpass him in melody—that bird which in flower-laden spring pours forth her dirge, uttering her honey-tongued song among the leaves. At that hour the clear-voiced nymphs accompany him, moving with nimble feet, singing beside some well of dark water, while Echo laments around the mountain top, and the god, now on this side of the chorus, now on that, or at times sidling into the middle, orders the dance powerfully with his feet.

On his back he wears a spotted lynx-pelt, and delights his heart with high-pitched songs in a lush meadow, where crocuses and sweet-scented hyacinths lie mingled amid the grass. They sing of the blessed gods of high Olympus, and tell of such a one as Hermes, the luck-bringer *par excellence*, and how he reached Arcadia, the land of countless springs, the mother of flocks, where lies his sacred precinct as god of Cyllene. For there, though a god, he used to pasture rough-coated sheep, in the service of a mortal, because there fell upon him and grew hot a melting desire to make love to the rich-tressed daughter of Dryops. And he consummated his love. And in the palace she bore to Hermes a dear son, from his birth a monstrous sight to look upon, with his goat's feet and twin horns, a noise-loving, merry-laughing creature. When she saw his uncouth features, his bearded chin, his mother was afraid, and she sprang up and fled, and left the child. Then luck-bringing Hermes received him, and took him in his arms; exceedingly glad in his heart was the god. And he went swiftly to the seats of the immortal gods, carrying his son wrapped in the thick pelt of a mountain hare, and set him down beside Zeus and the other immortal gods, and displayed his son. Then all the Immortals were glad at heart, and Bacchic Dionysus above all the rest; and they called him Pan, because he delighted all their hearts. So hail to you, Lord! I seek your favour with a song. And now I shall remember you and another song as well.

II(d) Sicilian summer

Theocritus, *Idyll* VII.128–57

So much I said: and Lycidas, laughing pleasantly as before, made me a present of his cudgel, as a token of friendship in the Muses. And he turned off to the left and took the road for Pyxa, but Eukritos and I and the fair Amyntas turned towards Phrasydamas' farm and bedded ourselves down happily on deep couches of soft rush and freshly clipped vine-leaves. Many a poplar and elm were swaying overhead, and near at hand the sacred water from the cave of the nymphs babbled as it flowed down the rocks. On the shady branches the dusky cicadas were busily chattering; and far away the tree-frog called in the dense thornbush. Larks and finches were singing, the dove was moaning, and bees flitted humming around the springs. Everything smelt of a rich harvest and the season of fruit.

Pears at our feet, and apples by our sides were rolling in abundance, and the boughs hung low to the ground with their weight of sloes. And the four-year seal was loosened from the cap of the wine-jars. Nymphs of Castalia that haunt the steep of Parnassus, was it a bowl like this that old Chiron served to Herakles in Pholus' rocky cavern? Was it nectar like this that set that shepherd beside the Anapus dancing among his sheepfolds, even the mighty Polyphemus who pelted ships with mountains?—such nectar as you Nymphs mixed for us to drink that day by the altar of Demeter of the threshing-floor. On her heap let me plant again the great winnowing-fork, while she smiles upon us with sheaves and poppies in either hand.

II(e) The man-made Italian landscape

Lucretius, *On the Nature of Things* v.1261–78

But the pattern for sowing and the start of grafting was made by the creative power of Nature herself, since berries and nuts as they fell from the trees in due season put forth swarms of shoots beneath. From nature too they got the desire to fasten grafts to branches, and to plant young saplings in the ground over the fields. Then they tried one way after another of filling their smiling plot, and saw wild fruits growing tame in the soil through tender care and loving tillage. And day by day they began to force the woods more and more to retreat into the hills, surrendering the land below to cultivation, so that on hills and plains they might have meadows, pools, streams, crops and smiling vineyards, and the blue-grey belt of olives might run between with a sharp dividing line, spreading over rises and hollows and plains; even as now you see the whole land marked out with a diversity of beauty, as men deck it out by planting it here and there with sweet fruit-trees, fencing it in by planting it all round with fruitful shrubs.

II(f) In praise of Italy

Varro, *On Farming* I.2

Contrast with this Italy, where every useful product not merely grows, but grows to perfection. What emmer is to be compared with Campanian, what wheat with Apulian, what wine with Falernian, what oil with Venafran? Is not Italy so planted up with fruit-trees that it looks like one great orchard? Is Phrygia, which Homer calls 'the vine-clad', more quickly covered with vines than this land? Or Argos, which the same poet calls 'the rich in grain', more covered in wheat? In what other land does the *iugerum** produce fifteen *cullei* † of wine, as some districts in Italy do?

---

*See p.20.n.　　　　　　　　　　　† 1 *Culleus* = 20 *amphorae* = *c.* 125 gallons.

II(g) In praise of Italy
Virgil, *Georgics* II.136–58; 173–7

But no, not Mede-land with its wealth of woods,
Nor Ganges fair, nor Hermus thick with gold,
Can match the praise of Italy; nor Ind,
Nor Bactria, nor Panchaia, one wide tract
Of incense-teeming sand. Here never bulls
With nostrils snorting fire upturned the sod
Sown with the monstrous dragon's teeth, nor crop
Of warriors bristled thick with lance and helm;
But heavy harvest and the Massic juice
Of Bacchus fill its borders, overspread
With fruitful flocks and olives. Hence arose
The war-horse stepping proudly o'er the plain;
Hence thy white flocks, Clitumnus, and the bull,
Of victims mightiest, which full oft have led,
Bathed in thy sacred stream, the triumph-pomp
Of Romans to the temples of the gods.
Here blooms perpetual spring, and summer here
In months that are not summer's; twice teem the flocks;
Twice doth the tree yield service of her fruit.
But ravening tigers come not nigh, nor breed
Of savage lion, nor aconite betrays
Its hapless gatherers, nor with sweep so vast
Doth the scaled serpent trail his endless coils
Along the ground, or wreathe him into spires.
Mark too her cities, so many and so proud,
Of mighty toil the achievement, town on town
Up rugged precipices heaved and reared,
And rivers undergliding ancient walls . . .

JAMES RHOADES
(Virgil, *The Georgics*, trans. James Rhoades,
London, 1881)

II(h) A landscaped haven
Virgil, *Aeneid* I.158–69

There, in a deep inlet, lies a place where an island forms a harbour locked in by its sides; not a wave from the open sea but breaks upon it, then divides in retreating channels. On either side great cliffs and twin crags tower heavenward, beneath whose summits stretches a wide expanse of still, sheltered water. Beyond the water is a background of shimmering woods, reaching down, and behind them an overhanging grove, dark with gloomy shade. Under the brow of the cliffs that front the entrance is a cave of stalactites; within, fresh water and seats cut in the living rock, for nymphs have their abode there. Here weary ships will never need a cable or a fluked anchor to bite and hold them fast.

II(j) A Tuscan villa and its setting

Pliny, *Letters* v.67.7–13

The landscape round here is really beautiful. Imagine some enormous amphitheatre that could only be the work of Nature. The broad, extensive plain is ringed by mountains, their summits topped by ancient groves of tall timber, where there is hunting in plenty and in variety. The mountain slopes are covered with plantations of timber, interspersed with large mounds of fertile soil (you will scarcely find rocks anywhere even if you search for them), which are no less rich than the most open plains, and which ripen crops as rich but which are harvested later in the season. Below these the vineyards extend on every side, weaving their uniform pattern far and wide. And where they end, shrubs spring up to form a sort of boundary at the foot. Then come the meadows and grain fields, which can only be broken by huge oxen and the most powerful ploughs. The soil is so stiff that at first ploughing it rises up in massive clods, needing nine ploughings to complete the breaking process. The meadows are ablaze with flowers, covered with clover and other tender plants, which are always soft and fresh, for everything is fed by perennial streams. But where the water collects in greatest quantity there is no marsh, because the ground is sloping, discharging into the Tiber any water it has received but not absorbed. The river, which cuts the fields in two, is navigable, and conveys all the produce to the city, but only in winter and spring—in summer its level drops, and the dried-up bed deprives it of its title of a great river, which it regains in the autumn. You will very much enjoy looking down on this stretch of countryside from the mountain; the view you will get will appear to be less of a real landscape, and more of a painted scene of surpassing beauty; and wherever you turn your eyes they will be refreshed with its variety and arrangement.

II(k) En route to a country estate
Pliny, *Letters* II.17.I

You are surprised that I'm so fond of my Laurentinum (or, if you like the name better), my Laurens; but you'll stop feeling surprised when you have discovered the charm of the villa, the convenience of its situation and the fine stretch of coast that it covers. It is a mere seventeen miles from Rome; so that, after finishing your chores in the city, you can spend the night here with a full day's work behind you. You can get here by two different routes, that via Laurentum and that via Ostia. If you take the Laurentum road you must turn off at the fourteenth milestone, if the Ostia at the eleventh. Both roads have sandy stretches, making the journey rather heavy and tedious for driving, but easy and pleasant for riding. The landscape on all sides is highly diversified; in some places the road is narrowed by woodlands closing in, elsewhere it opens out into broad stretches of pasture, where large flocks of sheep and herds of horses and cattle, driven down from the mountains by the severe winter weather, grow sleek in the vernal warmth.

II(l) River scenes
Ausonius, *The Moselle* 23–47; 189–208

Hail, river blessed by the fields, blessed by the farmers, to whom the Belgae owe the honour of imperial favour! River, whose hills are planted up with yoked vines of fragrant Bacchus. Your banks, O verdant stream, are packed with turf. Ship-bearer, like the sea, gliding down with sloping waters, as befits a river, and with your crystal depths counterfeiting lakes; nay more, you match the brooks for hurrying flow, and outmatch cool springs for limpid draughts. In your oneness you yet include all that belongs to springs, brooks, rivers, lakes, and tidal ocean's ebb and flow. As you glide on with unruffled waters you feel neither the murmur of the breeze nor the commotion from hidden rocks, nor are you forced by overpowering shoals to hurry on in swirling rapids; no islets have you in midstream to interrupt your course—lest the glory of your well-earned title be removed by some island that breaks and splits your flow. You have been granted two means of voyaging: one, when boats sail downstream with following current, and their speeding oars strike the churned-up water; the other, when, along the banks, the tow-rope never slackening, the bargemen take on their shoulders the strain of the hawsers fastened to the masts. For yourself, how often do you wonder at the windings of your stream, thinking that its natural speed moves almost too sluggishly! No mud-grown sedge fringes your banks, nor do you spread filthy ooze about your margin; feet tread quite dry to the water's edge . . .

There is a sight for all to enjoy, when the sparkling river mirrors the shady hillside, the waters of the stream seem to be in leaf, and the river to be overgrown with vine-shoots. What a splendid colour envelops the waters when the evening star has driven the shadows forward, and bathes the Moselle in the verdant mountain! Whole hills float in the shimmering ripples; here quivers the distant tendril, and here the ripe cluster swells in the glassy flood. The cheated boatman counts the green vines—the boatman whose bark-covered skiff floats on the level flood out in midstream, when the painted hill merges with the water, and the river knits up the edges of the shadows.

How pleasing is the pageant presented by this sight, when in mock-battle the oared skiffs fight in midstream, and circle in and out, grazing the sprouting turf of the cropped fields along the banks! The farmer, standing where the green bank rises up, watches the quick-moving owners as they leap about on stern or prow, and the young crewman, wandering over the river's wide expanse, nor ever feels the day is slipping by, but puts *their* play before *his* business; and fresh delight shuts out old cares.

II(m) Squillace and its surroundings

Cassiodorus, *Miscellany* VIII.31

In its situation overlooking the Adriatic Sea, the city hangs upon the hills like a cluster of grapes, hills that swell up, but not so as to make them hard to climb, but high enough to afford a delightful prospect over the verdant plains and the deep blue back of the sea. The city beholds the rising sun from its very cradle. The oncoming day sends out no Aurora as herald, but with a single burst lights up its torch, and the brightness quivers on high. She looks upon the sun-god as he rejoices, and basks in his brightness all day long; and so she has the more rightful claim to be his birthplace, putting that of Rhodes in the shade. The city enjoys clear skies, and is endowed with a temperate climate; she enjoys sunny winters and cool summers, and life goes on without unhappiness, where there is no fear of inhospitable weather. Here men have greater freedom of emotions, since moderation rules all things. A hot country makes its children sharp-witted and changeable, a cold one makes them sluggish and deceitful; it is only a temperate climate which endows men with its own peculiar quality. That is why the ancients called Athens the seat of the wise, for their city, bathed in pure air, with lavish hand prepared their clear-sighted minds for the con-templative role. Is there no difference then between absorbing muddy waters into your bodies and drinking in the limpidity of a spring of very sweet water? Thus the strength of the spirit is burdened, when it is crushed by heavier spirit. We shall inevitably submit to such influences, since clouds depress us, and clear skies naturally make us glad once again, for the essence of our heavenly spirit rejoices at everything that is unwrought and unpolluted. Squillace also enjoys a full share of sea delicacies, possessing nearby those 'Gates of Neptune' which I myself constructed. At the foot of Mount Moscius I excavated a space in the bowels of the rocks, and in a suitable manner let in the waters of Nereus, where a school of fishes sporting in their free captivity both refreshes the spirit with pleasure, and charms the eye with wonder. They rush eagerly to the hand, and before they are turned into food, demand morsels. There man feeds the darling creatures, and, while he has his catch within his grasp, it often happens that when he has fished his fill he leaves them untouched. While quietly resting in the city, the inhabitants are not deprived of the sight of men working happily in the fields. Here can be seen the full vineyards, bumper crops on the threshing-floor, and there the dark-green olive shows her face. No one lacks the pleasure of the countryside, who has the opportunity to see it all from the city. Since the latter has virtually no walls, you may think of it as a rural city, or you may adjudge it to be an urban farm, and since it lies between the one and the other, it is known to enjoy high praise.

II(n) A voyage along the Italian coast

Rutilius Namatianus, *On His Return* 220–38; 345–68

(a) In the half light of dawn the anchor was lifted.
As we left the shoreline the colours were
Returning and we could see the fields of the hills.
Our little vessels stayed close to the shore
So that safety was always near. The cargo ships,
With their huge spread of sail, can plough the waves
Of summer but we chose autumn for its still air
Because it permitted us to escape
The land without in the least impeding our haste.
We sailed north past Alsium, and Pyrgi
Was soon behind us. Today these are large estates;
At one time they were little villages.
Caere, once called Agylla, passed on our right,
And then we passed Castrum, a ruin now,
Destroyed by wind and water; only a gateway
Marks the place where men lived. Over that gate
Like a guardian, is the figure of a shepherd
With horns on his brow. Time has forgotten
His name, though legend associates it with Pan.

(b) We anchored near the shore and measured out the beach
For camp. A grove of myrtle gave us wood,
We pitched our tents on oars that we used for tent poles.

Daylight returned. We pushed on in the calm
And, though it did not seem to move, the fading shore
Proved that our bow was slowly progressing.
Soon Ilva came into sight. It is a rich place
With more iron in its rocks than Noricum.
Iron from Ilva is even purer than that made
In Gaul by the Bituriges although
The island has fuel for only the smallest hearths.
Sardinian ore is also poorer.
The earth does more good by giving birth to iron
Than it does with all its rivers of gold.
Gold begets vice; the desire of gold leads to crime.
Golden gifts make brides of unwilling girls;
Loyalty tainted by gold can betray a town;
Gold frees ambition to do as it will.
But this is not true of iron; iron ploughs barren fields;
Iron provides man's first occupation;
The demi-gods mastered nature with iron weapons;
Iron gives a man the strength of many men.
With thoughts like these I passed a quiet time while we
Listen to the chief oarsman calling strokes.

HAROLD ISBELL
(*The Last Poets of Imperial Rome*,
Harmondsworth, 1971)

III

THE COUNTRY THROUGH
THE EYE OF THE TOWNSMAN

Quot homines, tot sententiae! The contents of this chapter cover a whole gamut of sentiments and attitudes. The relationships between town and country were never static; the advance of urbanized society and the increasing acceptance of its refinements turn yesterday's paragon of rustic virtue into today's clodhopper (see Ch. I e and f). As for the countryside itself, attitudes naturally varied according to economic and social relationships with the land, but striking contrasts may be noticed between persons of the same rank. The central figures in III a and III c both belong to the important class of absentee landowners; but whereas Xenophon's gentleman farmer has much in common with a typical English squire, who takes an intelligent interest in the work of the estate, but also finds opportunity to practise his riding, Cato's model owner has no time for such frivolities: he has his programme full from the moment of his arrival, beginning with a thoroughgoing survey, followed by a series of searching questions to his manager, and a detailed comparison of the progress made since his last visit, after which the manager will have to account for any discrepancies! In II(d) Cicero presents a different Cato: mellowed now by age, he dwells lovingly on the pleasures of farming, especially those of vine-growing.

In the *Satires* and *Letters* of Horace—the freedman's son, who had an intimate knowledge of both town and country, and from the upper and lower ranges of the social spectrum—our theme is handled with skill, subtlety and of course with humour. In Epode 11 (Ch. III e) he pays an eloquent tribute to the work and leisure of the sturdy independent farmer, only to shock the unsuspecting reader at the end by placing these sentiments into the mouth of a man who could not possibly sustain the desired role, namely a city moneylender! The theme of III(g), a letter to his farm manager, is common, indeed hackneyed: 'You were a slave in Rome, and discontented; now you've got your wish, you pine for the taverns and the whores'. The theme is conventional: not so the treatment; instead of lecturing the man, Horace tells him how he himself has come to terms with life and achieved happiness (I follow Fränkel's interpretation against the common view of this Letter as a conventional sermon (*Horace*, 310–14). The tale of the two mice is the concluding portion of a beautifully balanced satire, the first half of which describes the poet's daily round in the city, its noise and rush and frustration. But the poem is not a straight piece of escapism, like III(n); and the writer lives in two worlds, and enjoys both (on this see Fränkel, 142–3). The remaining items call for no particular comment; the

36

Seneca (Ch. III l) is unusually direct and down-to-earth, with no more than a single sentence of moralizing!

III(a) A day on a suburban Greek farm

Xenophon, *Oeconomicus* XI

'Well then, Socrates, said Ischomachus, 'I have been in the habit of getting up at a time of day when, if I happened to want to pay anyone a visit, I should find him still at home. And if I have any business to do in the city, I make this serve as a walk; but if there's nothing important going on in town, my servant leads my horse in front of me into the country, and I use that journey as perhaps a better form of exercise than I should get walking about in the arcade. And after I've arrived on the farm, whether I happen to find them planting, or ploughing the fallow, or sowing or harvesting a crop, I watch how each of these operations is being performed, and change the method, if I have a better one to suggest than the one they're using. After this I usually mount my horse, and practise riding, following as closely as I can the riding required in actual warfare, and dodging neither a sideways slope nor steep ground nor ditches nor canals. However I take every possible care not to lame my horse while he is doing this. When this is over my servant leads the horse home after letting him have a roll, at the same time bringing to town from the farm anything we need. I make my way home sometimes at a walking pace, sometimes running, and give myself a dry bath. And then, Socrates, I take for my morning meal just enough to get through the day without either an empty or an overburdened stomach.

III(b) Ill temper on the farm

Menander, *The Bad-Tempered Man*

PYRRHIAS: I'm certain he's coming back to have another go at me! By Zeus, I tell you, Sostratos, we'll all be slaughtered!
SOSTRATOS: No you won't! Now just tell me carefully exactly what you said when you spoke to him.
P: I can't, I'm all of a dither, and out of breath.
S (*getting a hold of him*): You'll tell me now.
P: Well, first I knocked on the door, and said I wanted to see the master. A wretched old bag emerged, and stood over there, where I was talking just

now, and pointed him out, up there on the hillside, walking round his confounded pear trees, collecting enough wood to make a gallows.

s: How awful! Go on, go on!

p: Well then, I went into the field and approached him. I thought I'd let him see that I was a decent, friendly sort of chap. I called out to him—I was still some distance away—and said: 'I've come to talk over some urgent business with you, sir; business of importance to you.' 'To hell with you!' says he; 'who gave you orders to enter my field?' With that he picks up a lump of turf and chucks it straight into my face!

CHAEREAS: The Hell! To blazes with him!

p: And as I blinked, and shouted, 'Poseidon drown you!', he picked up a stick this time, and thrashed me with it, bawling out 'What business have you got with me?' at the top of his voice, and then, 'Don't you know where the public road is?'

CH (to Sostratos): This farmer pal of yours is absolutely bonkers!

p: In the end I hopped it. He chased me for nearly two miles, right round the hill, and then down here through the thorn-brake, pelting me first with turves and stones, and then with his pears, when he'd nothing else to throw. He's an absolute old curmudgeon, a holy terror! Come out of here, please!

s: I'm not afraid of him.

III(c) Farm management for the absentee owner

Cato, On Farming II

When the master arrives at his country estate, after paying his respects to the household god, let him go round the whole farm, if possible on the day of arrival; if not, at least on the following day. When he has found out how the field operations have progressed, what has been completed, and what still remains to be done, let him summon his overseer the next day, and ask him what part of the work has been completed, and what has still to be done; whether the jobs have been finished in good time, and whether he can finish the remainder within the stipulated time, and what were the returns of wine, wheat and other products. Having obtained all this information, he must calculate the time and labour consumed. If the amount of work done seems inadequate, but the overseer reports that he himself has done his very best, but that the slaves have been sick, the weather bad, slaves have absconded, he has had public work to do, when he has given many such excuses and others like them, you must recall the overseer to the estimate of the work done and the labourers employed. If it has been a rainy period, remind him of the jobs that could have been done on rainy days: cleaning and pitching the storage jars, cleaning out the farmstead, shifting grain, hauling out manure, making a manure pit, cleaning seed, mending old harness, and making new; that the labourers should have mended their smocks and hoods. Remind him also that on feast days old ditches could have been cleaned, roads repaired, briers cut down, the garden dug over, a meadow weeded, faggots bundled, thorns rooted up, emmer pounded, and a general clean-up done. When the slaves were sick their rations should have been reduced. When all this information has been collected calmly, give orders for the remaining jobs to be completed; run over the accounts for cash, grain and fodder; go over the wine accounts, the oil accounts, reckoning up what has been sold, what paid for, what has still to be collected, and what saleable items are left over. Satisfactory guarantees of payment should be accepted; the balance remaining should be checked up. Give orders that any shortfall in this year's supply should be made up, and any surplus sold. Whatever needs to be put out to contract should be contracted for. The owner should give orders and leave them in writing concerning any work that he wants done, and any work that is to be put out on contract. He should review the livestock, hold an auction and, if he can get his price, sell the oil, the wine and the surplus grain; let him sell the worn-out oxen, blemished cattle, blemished sheep, the wool, the hides, old wagons, worn-out implements, old slaves, sickly slaves, and anything else that is surplus to his requirements. The owner should acquire the selling habit, not the buying habit.

III(d) The pleasures of farming

Cicero, *On Old Age* xv.52–4

I now come to the pleasures of farming, in which I take unbelievable delight; for age is no obstacle to them, and in my opinion they come nearest to the life of wisdom. Their dealings are with the earth, which never rejects control, and never returns without interest what she has received, but always with a return, which is sometimes rather small, but usually considerable. What I enjoy however is not the crop alone, but the soil itself, its nature and its power. It takes the scattered grains of wheat within its soft, upturned bosom, hides it there at first out of sight (it is hidden by 'harrowing', a word meaning to 'hide'); then, having warmed it with the heat of its embrace, expands it and from it draws forth the verdant blade, which, supported by its fibrous roots, grows gradually to maturity, and stands erect upon its jointed stalk, enclosed within a sheath, when now it attains manhood, so to speak. And when it emerges from the sheath, it puts forth its fruit in the ear, built up in rows and protected by a palisade of spikes against the attacks of the smaller birds.

Why should I mention the origin, planting and growth of the vine? To give you an idea of the genuine pleasure and recreation of my old age I cannot exhaust the pleasures of vine-growing. I pass over the inner power of all these things which are generated by the earth, a power that, from the tiny seed of the fig or grape-stone, or from the smallest seeds of other fruits and plants can give birth to such enormous trunks and branches; do not mallet-shoots, suckers, cuttings, divisions and layers move any man to wonder and delight? The vine, whose nature is to droop, and which falls to the ground unless it is propped, raises itself by means of its finger-like tendrils, gripping the props, and as it multiplies its trailing growth the skilful husbandman checks its growth by pruning with the knife, lest the shoots run to wood and spread too far in all directions. So in early spring, the branches left at every joint bring forth a bud, whence appears the grape, the off-spring of this bud, and burgeons with the moisture of the earth and the heat of the sun; at first it is very bitter to the taste, but afterwards, as it ripens, it becomes sweet, and, clothed in foliage, it has no lack of moderate warmth, and wards off the violent heat of the sun. Can anything be more delicious to the taste, and more beautiful to the eye?

III(e) Daydreams of a moneylender

Horace, *Epodes* 11

'A man is happy when, far from the business world,
  like the earliest tribe of men
he cultivates the family farm with his team,
  and is free from usury's ties
(not as a soldier, stirred by the trumpet's wild cry,
  nor quaking in an angry sea),
when he keeps away from the Forum and the proud
  doorways of influential men.
This is his life: when the shoots of his vines mature,
  he marries them to tall poplars,
or, in a secluded valley, he looks over
  his lowing cattle as they graze,
and pruning away useless branches with his hook,
  grafts more fruitful ones to the trees,
or he puts up pressed honey in his well-scrubbed jars
  or shears the struggling, helpless sheep;
above all, when through his lands autumn lifts his head
  with a crown of ripening fruit,
how delighted he is, plucking the grafted pears
  and the purple cluster of grapes
as your offering, Priapus, and Silvanus,
  protector of boundary lines.
How pleasant to rest, sometimes beneath an old oak,
  sometimes on a carpet of grass;
all the while the brook glides by between its high banks,
  the birds are trilling in the trees,
and the splashing waters of springs play counterpoint,
  a summons to easy slumber.

But when the time of winter and thunderous Jove
   comes on with its rain and its snow,
with his pack of hounds from here, from there, he forces
   the fierce boars towards the ready nets,
or stretches a wide-meshed net on its polished pole,
   a snare for the greedy thrushes,
and the trembling rabbit and the far-flying crane
   he traps in his noose, a good catch.
Who would not forget, in such a life, the sorrows
   and cares that accompany love?
But if a chaste wife would do her part in caring
   for the home and the dear children,
like a Sabine woman or the sunburned wife of
   a strong Apulian farmer,
would pile seasoned firewood beside the sacred hearth
   for her weary husband's return,
and shutting the frisky flock in their wattled pen,
   would milk their swollen udders dry,
and bringing out this year's wine, still sweet in its cask,
   would prepare a home-cooked supper,
I could not be more pleased by Lake Lucrine oysters,
   or by turbot or by scarfish,
should winter as it roars over Eastern waters
   drive some of them near our seacoast;
no African hen or Ionian pheasant
   would make its way to my belly
more enjoyably than olives chosen from the
   ripest branches in the orchard,
or leaves of meadow-loving sorrel and mallows
   that are good for a sick body,
or a lamb slaughtered on the Feast of Boundaries,
   or a kid retrieved from a wolf.
How delightful, at such a feast, to see the flock
   hurrying home from the pasture,
to see the worn-out oxen as with weary necks
   they drag along the upturned plough
and the homebred slaves, that crowd a rich house, in place
   about the gleaming household gods.'
When Alfius the usurer had said all this,
   on the brink of a country life,
he collected all of his money on the Ides,
   invested it on the Calends.

J. P. CLANCY

III(f) Every man to his trade

Horace, *Letters* 1.7.46–59; 71–98

Philip, whose youth was spent in feats of war,
Now grown a famous lawyer at the bar,
Returning from the courts one sultry day,
Complain'd, how tedious was the lengthen'd way
To folks in years; then wistfully survey'd
A new-trimm'd spark, who, joying in the shade,
Loll'd in a barber's shop, with ease reclin'd,
And pared his nails, right indolent of mind.
'Demetrius (so was call'd his favourite slave,
For such commissions a right-trusty knave),
Run and inquire of yonder fellow straight,
His name, friends, country, patron, and estate.'
    He goes, returns, and—'Menas is his name;
Of moderate fortune, but of honest fame;
A public crier, who a thousand ways
Bustles to get, and then enjoys his ease.
A boon companion 'mongst his equals known,
And the small house he lives in is his own.
His business over, to the public shows,
Or to the field of Mars, he sauntering goes.'
    Methinks, I long to see this wondrous wight.
Bid him be sure to sup with me tonight . . .
. . . Behold him now at supper, where he said,
Or right or wrong, what came into his head.
When Philip saw his eager gudgeon bite,
At morn an early client, and at night
A certain guest, a project to complete,
He takes him with him to his country-seat.
On horseback now he ambles at his ease,
The soil, the climate, his incessant praise.
    Philip, who well observ'd our simple guest,
Laughs in his sleeve, resolv'd to have his jest
At any rate; then lends him fifty pounds,
And promis'd fifty more, to buy a spot of ground,
    But, that our tale no longer be delay'd,
Bought is the ground, and our spruce merchant made
A very rustic; now, at endless rate,
Vineyards and furrows are his constant prate.
He plants his elms for future vines to rise,

Grows old with care, and on the prospect dies.
But when his goats by sickness, and by thieves
His sheep are lost, his crop his hope deceives
When his one ox is kill'd beneath the yoke,
Such various losses his best spirits broke.
At midnight dragging out his only horse,
He drives to Philip's house his desperate course;
Who, when he saw him rough, deformed with hair,
'Your ardent love of pelf, your too much care
Hath surely brought you to this dismal plight.—'
Oh! call me wretch, if you would call me right,
But let this wretch your clemency implore,
By your good genius; by each heavenly power;
By that right hand, sure never pledg'd in vain,
Restore to me my former life again.
To his first state let him return with speed,
Who sees how far the joys he left exceed
His present choice: for all should be confin'd
Within the bounds which nature hath assign'd.

PHILIP FRANCIS
(Horace, *Satires and Epistles*, trans.
Philip Francis, London, 1747)

III(g) The poet addresses his town-loving farm manager

Horace, *Letters* I.14

Thou steward of the woods and country-seat,
That give me to myself; whose small estate,
Which you despise, five worthy fathers sent,
One from each house, to Varia's parliament.
Let us enquire, if you with happier toil
Root out the thorns and thistles of the soil,
Than Horace tears his follies from his breast;
Whether my farm or I be cultivated best,
Though Lamia's pious tears, that ceaseless mourn
His brother's death, have hindered my return,
Thither my warmest wishes bend their force,
Start from the goal, and beat the distant course.
Rome is your rapture, mine the rural seat;
Pleas'd with each other's lot, our own we hate;

But both are fools, and fools in like extreme;
Guiltless the place, that we unjustly blame,
For in the mind alone our follies lie,
The mind, that never from itself can fly.
A slave at Rome, and discontented there,
A country life was once your silent prayer:
A rustic grown, your first desires return;
For Rome, her public games and baths, you burn.
More constant to myself, I leave with pain,
By hateful business forced, the rural scene.
From different objects our desires arise,
And thence the distance that between us lies;
For what you call inhospitably drear,
To me with beauty and delight appear.
Full well I know a tavern's greasy stream,
And a vile stew, with joy your heart inflame,
While my small farm yields rather herbs than vines,
Nor there a neighbouring tavern pours its wines,
Nor harlot-minstrel sings, when the rude sound
Tempts you with heavy heels to thump the ground.
But you complain, that with unceasing toil
You break, alas! the long unbroken soil,
Or loose the wearied oxen from the plough,
And feed with leaves new-gathered from the bough.
Then feels your laziness an added pain,
If e'er the rivulet be swoln with rain;
What mighty mounds against its force you rear,
To teach its rage the sunny mead to spare!
Now hear, from whence our sentiments divide;
In youth, perhaps with not ungraceful pride,
I wore a silken robe, perfumed my hair,
And without presents charmed the vernal fair;
From early morning quaffed the flowing glass;
Now a short supper charms, or on the grass
To lay me down at some fair river's side,
And sweetly slumber as the waters glide.
Nor do I blush to own my follies past,
But own, those follies should no longer last.
None there with eye askance my pleasures views,
With hatred dark or poison'd spite pursues;
My neighbours laugh to see with how much toil
I carry stones, or break the stubborn soil.
You with my city-slaves would gladly join,
And on their daily pittance hardly dine;

While more refined they view with envious eye
The gardens, horses, fires that you enjoy.
Thus the slow ox would gaudy trappings claim;
The sprightly horse would plough amongst the team;
By my advice let each with cheerful heart,
As best he understands, employ his art.

PHILIP FRANCIS
(Horace, *Satires and Epistles*, trans.
Philip Francis, London, 1747)

III(h) The tale of the town mouse and the country mouse

Horace, *Satires* II.6.77–117

In the middle of all this dinner-table discussion my neighbour Cervius is churning out old wives' tales, but all very much to the point. When some witless ass praises Arellius with his wealth and his worries, he kicks off like this:

'Once upon a time, as the story goes, the Country Mouse entertained the Town Mouse in his wretched hole. The two were very old friends. The Country Mouse lived rough and kept a tight hold on his store-cupboard, but he could still ease off when he played host. The gist of the story is that he made free of his stored-up chickpeas and long-grained oats, and served up in his own mouth some desiccated berries and half-chewed scraps of bacon-fat, resolved to overcome with this varied menu the jaded palate of his guest. But the Town Mouse merely picked at each separate morsel with disdainful tooth, while the master of the house lay stretched out on this year's straw, eating emmer and darnel, leaving the choicer dainties to his guest. At last the Town Mouse turned to the Country Mouse and said: "My dear chap, what possible joy are you getting out of living on the ridge of this wooded precipice? Won't you rate me and the city way above these barbarous woods? Put yourself in my hands and, with me at your side, clear out of here. Earth-born creatures have been given mortal souls, and there's no escape from death for great or small. Live it up then, my dear chap, while you have the chance and, while you live, never forget you haven't a long innings of it!" With these remarks he won over the Country Mouse, who leapt jauntily forth from his house, and the pair of them pursued their journey as planned, eager to creep inside the city walls under cover of the night. And now night already occupied the midmost space of heaven when together they set foot in a wealthy mansion, where the coverlets, dyed scarlet in oak-berry juice, shone resplendent on the ivory couches, with many a course left over from the banquet of the night before, standing there in towering baskets. Then his host set the Country Mouse lolling on the scarlet draperies,

45

while himself, in bustling waiter style, kept the banquet going without a break, tasting every dish before he served it. The Country Mouse, thrilled at his change of fortune, lay back at his ease, playing the well-fed guest amid the cheer, when suddenly a terrible banging of doors tumbled both mice off their couches. They ran in terror the length of the saloon, and still more panic-stricken were they when the lofty hall resounded with the baying of Molossian hounds. Then said the rustic: "I have no use for this style of living, and so, farewell! My woods and my cave, secure from snares, shall comfort me with thin vetch." '

III(j) In winter choose the pleasures of the town

Horace, *Odes* 1.9

See how Soracte stands with glistening depth of snow!
And how the straining woods can scarce support
Their burden, and the streams
Have frozen stiff with biting cold.

Thaw out the icy chill, my Thaliarchus,
By stacking up the hearth with logs,
And with generous hand fetch down
A Sabine amphora of wine four years in cask.

All else leave to the gods;
As soon as they have brought to rest
The winds that battle with the seething seas,
Nor cypresses, nor ancient ash-trees are any longer shaken.

Give up enquiring what tomorrow will bring forth;
And every day that Chance allows you
Put down to your credit, while you're young,
Nor scorn the sweet loving nor the dances,

While whining age is far away.
Now's the time for the playing-field and public squares,
And gentle whispering at nightfall
At the appointed hour of meeting.

Now too the time for the merry tell-tale giggle
Of the girl-friend lurking in the corner;
The time to snatch a prize from her arm
Or half-protesting finger.

III(k) Philemon and Baucis entertain the gods

Ovid, *Metamorphoses* VIII. 640–80

So, when the gods came to this little cottage,
Ducking their heads to enter, the old man
Pulled out a rustic bench for them to rest on,
As Baucis spread a homespun cover for it,
And then she poked the ashes around a little,
Still warm from last night's fire, and got them going
With leaves and bark, and blew at them a little,
Without much breath to spare, and added kindling,
The wood split fine, and the dry twigs, made smaller
By breaking them over the knee, and put them under
A copper kettle, and then she took the cabbage
Her man had brought from the well-watered garden,
And stripped the outer leaves off. And Philemon
Reached up, with a forked stick, for the side of bacon,
That hung below the smoky beam, and cut it,
Saved up so long, a fair-sized chunk, and dumped it
In the boiling water. They made conversation
To keep the time from being too long, and brought
A couch with willow frame and feet, and on it
They put a sedge-grass mattress, and above it
Such drapery as they had, and did not use
Except on great occasions. Even so,
It was pretty worn, it had only cost a little
When purchased new, but it went well enough
With a willow couch. And so the gods reclined.
Baucis, her skirts tucked up, was setting the table
With trembling hands. One table-leg was wobbly;
A piece of shell fixed that. She scoured the table
Made level now, with a handful of green mint,
Put on the olives, black or green and cherries
Preserved in dregs of wine, endive and radish,
And cottage cheese, and eggs, turned over lightly
In the warm ash, with shells unbroken. The dishes
Of course, were earthenware, and the mixing bowl
For wine was the same silver, and the goblets
Were beech, the inside coated with yellow wax.
No time at all, and the warm food was ready,
And wine brought out, of no particular vintage,
And pretty soon they had to clear the table

For the second course; here there were nuts and figs
And dates and plums and apples in wide baskets—
Remember how apples smell?—and purple grapes
Fresh from the vines, and a white honeycomb
As centerpiece, and all around the table
Shone kindly faces, nothing mean or poor
Or skimpy in good will.

ROLFE HUMPHRIES
(Ovid, *Metamorphoses*, trans. Rolfe
Humphries, Bloomington, Indiana, 1973)

III(1) On the simple life

Seneca, *Letters* LXXXVII

I've been shipwrecked even before embarking. How this happened I refrain from adding, in case you might think the affair should be included in the list of Stoic paradoxes; as for the latter, I'll demonstrate to you whenever you like, or even if you don't, that not one of them is false, nor yet so astonishing as it looks at first glance. In the meantime this trip has taught me how many superfluous items we had, and how, by making a resolve, we could get rid of things the removal of which we never feel when they are removed unavoidably. With a handful of slaves who could be accommodated in a single vehicle, with no belongings except what we carried on our backs, my friend Maximus and I have been spending two absolutely blissful days. On the ground lies a mattress, and on the mattress yours truly. We have two greatcoats, one of which has been converted into a blanket, the other into a coverlet. Our lunch has been minimal (it took no more than an hour to prepare).

One standing course of dried figs, and another of notebooks! The figs serve as a salad if I have bread, and as bread if I've none. They make each day a New Year's Day for me, and I make it prosperous and lucky by thinking good thoughts and cultivating a generous spirit, which is at its best when it has set aside all that doesn't belong to it, and won tranquillity by fearing nothing, and wealth by coveting nothing. The conveyance I'm driving in is a country cart; the mules show they're alive only by their walk; the muleteer goes barefoot, but not because it's summer. I can hardly persuade myself to want that contraption to be called mine. I still possess a wrong-headed bashfulness about doing right, and when we come across any well-heeled outfit, I blush in spite of myself, a sure sign that the principles I approve and applaud are still not solidly entrenched in me. The man who blushes for a shabby turn-out will boast of a smart one. I'm still backward. I haven't yet acquired the guts to advertise my plain living.

III(m) The townsman looks at country life

Juvenal, *Satires* III.160–80

The needy sons of Romulus should long ago have turned their backs on Rome. It is hard for men to rise whose worth is crushed by pinching poverty, but at Rome their struggle is harder than elsewhere. What a price for the meanest lodging! What a price for servants' rations! What a price for a modest little dinner! And here you blush to eat off earthenware, which you will deny is any disgrace, if suddenly transported to live among the Marsi or eat at a Sabine board. There, too, you'd be well content to wear the green country cape. Over much of Italy, if we'll only admit the truth, nobody wears the toga till he's dead. And even when they keep the solemn rites of festival days in a sward-made theatre, and when the favourite farce now comes on the boards once more, and the peasant's baby, in its mother's bosom, shrinks back in terror at the pale mask with its grinning mouth, you'll see a uniform dress for reserved seats and populace alike, even the high and mighty village bigwigs content themselves with white tunics, as the garb of their exalted office.

III(n) Country preferred to town

Martial, *Epigrams* XII.57

Do you ask why I often make for my little farm in arid Nomentum, and the untidy household of my villa? In the city, Sparsus, poor men have no place where they can think or stay quiet. Life is denied you in the morning by schoolmasters, at night by bakers, and all day long by the coppersmiths' hammers. Over here the money changer idly rattles on his dirty table a heap of Nero's coins; over there the hammerer of Spanish gold-dust beats his well-worn stone with burnished mallet, and Bellona's raving mob keeps it up, and so does the talkative shipwrecked seaman with his bandaged body, and the Jew his mother taught to beg, and the blear-eyed match-seller. The man who can reckon the losses lazy sleep must bear will say how many brass pots are clashed by city hands when the moon in her eclipse takes a drubbing from the Colchian wheel. You, Sparsus, know nothing of all this, nor can you know, lolling in the comfort of your Petillian domain, whose ground floor looks down on the hilltops, and where you have country in the city, and a Roman to dress your vines (the slopes of Falernus bear no greater crop), and inside your boundary a wide drive for your chaise, unfathomed depths of slumber, and a stillness that no tongue disturbs, nor any daylight unless you let it in. As for me, the laughter of the passing crowd wakes me up, and Rome is at the head of my couch. Whenever I'm worn out with anxiety, and want to sleep, I go to my farm.

IV

FARM MANAGEMENT AND THE FARMER'S CALENDAR

This chapter is almost entirely taken up with the practical aspects of farming. The first three passages, which deal with aspects of management and economics, require little comment. Xenophon's incentive bonus schemes for farmhands (Ch. IV b) may appear somewhat naïve, but were probably effective under prevailing conditions, and Varro's observations (Ch. IV c) on marketing facilities and interchange of surplus products with neighbouring farmers are of some interest (see my *Farm Equipment of the Roman World*, 1975), while his suggestion that the more energetic workmen should be consulted about the work programme has a distinctly modern ring! The remainder of the chapter is concerned with the all-important topic of the seasons and the activities appropriate to them, together with that of weather signs, the ancient precursors of our more sophisticated methods of forecasting, which help the farmer to save a valuable crop, or make an advantageous sowing. Hesiod and Virgil are the dominant contributors: indeed, the title of the former's poem *The Works and Days* might well have stood at the head of this and the following chapter, since between them they cover the entire range of agricultural operations. The link between 'Works' and 'Days' is a very close one: within the broad pattern of the seasons the Mediterranean farmer must watch closely for weather-signs—two-thirds of Virgil's *First Georgic* is devoted to them (see L. A. S. Jermyn, 'Weather-signs in Virgil', *Greece and Rome*, 1951), and Palladius' handbook on agriculture is itself a complete calendar of operations set out month by month. Hesiod's *Leaves from a Boeotian Farmer's Diary* (Ch. IV h) shows how strong was the influence of superstition in the form of lucky and unlucky days. Also included in this section is a 'standard' Roman almanac preserved on a large square block, each side of which contains three monthly columns of information and directions (Ch. IV k). It came to light in the garden of a house in the Campus Martius at Rome in 1550.

IV(a) Letters from Roman Egypt

Fayum Papyrus III (*c.* A.D. 100); Fayum Papyrus 119 (*c.* A.D.100)

1. Lucius Bellenus Gemellus to his own Epagathus, greeting! I blame you very much. You lost two little pigs through the exhaustion caused by the journey, although you had in the village ten animals fit for work. Heraklidas the ass-driver charged you with this, saying you told him to drive the pigs on foot ... They say lotus seed is eighteen drachmas in Dionysias. Whatever you may find the price to be, buy the twenty *artabae* ★ of lotus seed: we need it badly. Get a move on with the flooding of all the orchards ... and water the row of trees in 'The Prophet'. Do not neglect to do this. Goodbye.

2. Lucius Bellenus Gemellus to his son Sabinus, greeting! Aunes, the donkey-driver has bought a rotten ... bundle of hay at twelve drachmas, not merely a tiny bundle, but rotten as well and completely decayed, like dung. Get Sabinus, the son of Psellus from Psinachis, who is with you, to bring to town a letter of the prefect to the *strategos* † Dionysius ... Where did you put the receipt for the hay, and the agreement for his loan of a mina? Send the key and tell me where they are, so that I can get them out in order to have them on hand if I have to settle accounts with him. Mind you do this. Look after yourself. Greetings to Epagathus and our intimate friends. Goodbye.

IV(b) On farm management

Xenophon, *Oeconomicus* XIII

'But when you succeed in impressing very strongly on someone', I said, 'that he must take in hand anything you want him to do, will a man like that be immediately capable of undertaking management, or will he have to acquire additional knowledge if he is going to be a competent farm manager?' 'Yes, to be sure,' said Ischomachus, 'he will still need to know both what is to be done, and when and how. Otherwise, what greater value would there be in having a manager without this knowledge than in having a doctor who certainly looked after his patient, visiting him early and late, but was quite ignorant of what treatment he should give in order to do him good?' 'But look here,' I said, 'suppose he also learns the way in which the work is to be done, will he still need anything in addition, or will he now be your fully qualified manager?' 'In my opinion,' he said, 'he must also learn how to control the labour force.' 'Is

---

★*artaba* dry measure, between 26 and 45 litres.   †*strategos* governor of an Egyptian nome.

it the case, then,' I said, 'that you are training the managers to be capable of controlling men?' 'I certainly try at any rate,' said Ischomachus. 'And how, please, in heaven's name,' I said, 'do you train them to be good controllers of men?' 'Quite easily, Socrates,' he said; 'perhaps you would even laugh if you were to hear.' 'But believe me,' I said, 'it is certainly no topic for laughter, Ischomachus. It is surely evident that the man who can make others fit to control men can also teach them to become capable of being masters over men; and whoever can train them to be masters can also train them to be kings. Consequently the man who can do this seems to me to deserve great praise, not ridicule.' 'Well now, Socrates,' he said, 'other living creatures learn to obey from these two things; first, from being punished whenever they try to disobey, and secondly from being treated well whenever they perform their services with zest. Colts, at all events, learn to submit to the horsebreaker through being given something pleasant when they show obedience, and by getting into trouble when they disobey, until the point is reached when they serve him according to his will. And puppies too, though vastly inferior to human beings both in intelligence and in power of expression, nevertheless learn in precisely the same way how to run round and round, to turn somersaults, and to do many other tricks. For whenever they are obedient they get something they want, but whenever they are careless, they are punished. It is possible to make men more obedient by word of mouth, by showing them that it is to their advantage to be obedient. With slaves however the training thought suitable only for wild animals is very effective in teaching them obedience. You can succeed in getting a lot out of them by gratifying their stomach in relation to its desires. Ambitious natures are stimulated by praise in addition. Some natures are just as hungry for praise as others are for food and drink. These methods, then, which I employ myself to make men more amenable, I teach to all those whom I wish to develop as managers, and I support their efforts in the following ways: I do not make all the clothing and shoes which I have to provide for the work force of the same quality, but make some inferior, and some of better quality, so that I can reward the more efficient workmen with the better articles, and give the inferior ones those of poorer quality. It seems to me that good workers get discouraged when they see that, although they were responsible for the work done, those who neither put out effort nor take risks when the need arises get the same treatment as themselves.'

IV(c) On agricultural economics

Varro, *On Farming* 1.16

There remains a second topic within the subject, which is concerned with things external to the farm. Now the immediate surroundings of a farm, owing to its close connection with them, are extremely important to the operation of the farm; this topic has the same number of aspects (namely four): Is the neighbourhood unsafe? Is there no place to which we can easily transport our produce, and from which we can produce what we need? Thirdly, are roads and rivers to convey the produce either absent or unsafe? And fourthly, is there anything on adjoining farms likely to do good or harm to ours?

The first of these questions, the security or insecurity of the neighbourhood, is important; for there is much first-class land which it does not pay to cultivate because of the brigandage carried on by neighbours, as in Sardinia near Oelies, and in Spain on the borders of Portugal. Farms that have close by a suitable means of transporting their products to market, and importing from there what is needed on the farm, are for that reason profitable. Many people have among their holdings farms for which they must import from elsewhere the corn or wine or any other item that is lacking; on the other hand there are a good many who have a surplus they must export. Thus close to the city it pays to cultivate gardens on a large scale, for example those that grow violets and roses and many other products that are in demand in the city; whereas it would not pay to raise such crops on a distant farm which has no available market for them. Again, if there are towns or villages in the neighbourhood, or even well stocked farms and country houses belonging to wealthy owners, from which you can buy cheaply what your farm requires, and to which you can sell your surplus—crops, for example, or poles or reeds—the farm will be more profitable than if they have to be fetched from a distance, and sometimes it is even more profitable than if you could produce these items on your own land. And so, for example, farmers prefer to have in the vicinity men whose services they can call upon on a yearly contract—doctors, fullers, smiths—rather than keep their own on the farm; often the death of one of these skilled men does away with the profit on the farm.

Rich owners of large estates look to their home resources to supply this section of the work force: where towns or villages are too far away, they provide themselves with smiths and other essential artisans, and keep them on the farm, to prevent the slave farm-hands leaving their work, and loafing about, turning working days into holidays instead of increasing the output of the land by getting on with their work. . . . The transport of produce makes this type of farm all the more profitable if there are roads on which carts can easily be driven, or navigable rivers close at hand. We know that both methods are used for inward and outward transport on many farms.

Again, the productivity of a farm is affected by the way your neighbour plants the boundary areas. If, for instance, he has an oak-grove running up to the common boundary, it would be wrong for you to plant olives alongside such a plantation, for these have a natural antipathy to it so great that your trees will not only be less fruitful, but will even try to escape from them, to the extent of bending inwards towards the farm, as vines usually do when planted near cabbages. Like oak-trees, large-size walnut trees planted closely near by make the border of your farm completely sterile.

IV(d) Personnel management on the farm

Varro, *On Farming* 1.17

I have now spoken of the four divisions of an estate that are connected with the
soil, and of the second four that are external to the estate, and yet are concerned
with its cultivation; I now turn to the instruments of tillage. These are divided
by some authorities into two parts; the personnel, and the supports without
which they cannot work the land. Others divide them into three categories;
that of instruments which are articulate, the inarticulate, and the mute. To the
first category belong slaves, to the second, cattle, to the third, wagons. All land
is cultivated by men, whether slaves, free men, or a combination of the two; by
free men, when they till the ground themselves, with the help of their families,
as most poor peasants do, or by free hired labourers, when major agricultural
operations like the vintage and the haymaking are carried out by hired gangs
of free labourers; and by those whom our countrymen called 'debtors' (*obaerati,
obaerarii*), who still exist in large numbers in Asia, Egypt and Illyricum. About
these in general I have this to say: It pays better in an unhealthy district to use
hired labourers rather than slaves, and in a healthy district too for the major
tasks on the farm, such as storing the products of the vintage or the harvest. On
the qualifications required of such hands Cassius writes as follows: You should
obtain workers who can stand heavy labour, not less than twenty-two years of
age, and quick to learn the work of the farm. You may form a judgement of
this by the way they carry out the rest of their orders, and by asking one of the
new hands what they used to do for their previous masters.

The slaves should be neither timid nor high spirited. Those who have charge
of them ought to be able to read and write, and have some smattering of
education; they should be honest, and older than the hands I have mentioned;
the latter will be more inclined to obey them than they will younger men. In
addition to this the most important asset in the supervisor is a knowledge of
farm operations; his duty is not merely to give orders, but to set an example, so
that his subordinates may imitate him, and realize that there is a good reason
for his pre-eminence over them—namely his superiority in knowledge. Nor
must an overseer be allowed to enforce his orders by the lash rather than by
words, if only the same result can be achieved. Don't acquire too many slaves
of the same nationality: this is a fertile source of domestic quarrelling.

You must sharpen the interest of your foremen by means of rewards and
take care to let them have some property of their own; and mates from among
their fellow-slaves to bear them children; this makes them steadier and more
attached to the farm. It is because of these family ties that slaves from Epirus
have a higher reputation and command a better price. You should win the
goodwill of the foremen by showing them some consideration; and the ordinary
labourers who surpass their fellows should be consulted about the work to be

done: such treatment will make them think that they are less looked down upon, and that they are held in some esteem by their master. They are induced to take more interest in their work by more generous treatment, e.g. by more liberal rations of food or clothing, by occasional exemption from work, or by permission to graze some stock of their own on the farm, or other concessions of this sort; so that, for those on whom some rather heavy task has been imposed, or some punishment inflicted in some way, they may be consoled and their goodwill and kindly feeling towards their master restored.

IV(e) Watch for weather signs: keep active

Hesiod, *Works and Days* 485–97

But if you are late with your ploughing, you still have a remedy. When the cuckoo first calls from the leaves of the oak, and gladdens every man to the ends of the earth; then on the third day after, if Zeus of his grace has sent a good rain that just fills the hoofprints of an ox—no more, late ploughers then will prosper even as those who ploughed early. But note these things attentively— mark at the time the signs of the grey spring's coming, and the seasonable shower. But walk past the smithy, and the crowded lounging-place, in winter when the cold keeps men from their tasks—even then an energetic fellow can still increase his store—lest the helpless poverty of a harsh winter seize you, and you chafe a swollen foot with a hand grown thin.

IV(f) The rigours of winter

Hesiod, *Works and Days* 504–26

But beware the month of Lenaion, ill days of bitter frost,
Days that would flay an ox, when the wide seas are tossed
By Boreas, blowing hard from the horse-pastures of Thrace,
And land and woodland bellow, as he wrenches from their place,
Amid the glens of the mountain, many an oak high-crowned,
Many a stalwart fir, and flings them to the ground,
Till the multitudinous forest shouts with a single cry.
Shivering under their bellies the tails of the wild beasts lie,
For all the fur that warms them—through the shaggiest breast it goes,
Through the hide of the ox himself that icy tempest blows,
And through the goats' lank hair—the fleece of the sheep alone
With its thick wool can baffle that blast from the northward blown.
It sets an old man running; and yet it cannot come
To the tender maiden sitting by her mother's side at home,

Of the golden Aphrodite as yet all unaware.
Ay, warm in an inner chamber—all limbs new-bathed, and fair
With olive oil—she lays her down and slumbers sweet
Through the winter days, when No-bones must stir and gnaw his feet
Alone in his fireless house, and the depths of his dismal den;
For never forth to pasture the low sun lights him then.

RICHMOND LATTIMORE
(Hesiod, *Works and Days*, trans.
Richmond Lattimore, Ann Arbor, 1959)

IV(g) Relax in the height of summer
Hesiod, *Works and Days* 571–94

But when House-carrier climbs from the ground up the cornstalks, fleeing from the heat the Seven Sisters bring, the time for digging vines is past; then is the time for whetting your sickles, and calling out your men. Avoid a seat in the shade, and do not lie abed till morning. Now, in the days of harvest, when the hot sun tans the skin, now's the time to be up and about, to win your sheaves. Rise at daybreak, so that your life will be free from need. Those early hours will speed one third of your labours of the day. Dawn speeds a man on his journey, and advances him in his work—dawn that every day, all the world over, sets many a traveller on the road, and puts the yoke once more on many an ox's neck.

But when the artichoke flowers—when the shrill cicada, with fast-quivering wing, sings through summer's crushing heat, and perched in the green leafage of a tree pours out his piercing notes, then wine is at its best, and goats are fattest, women most randy, and men at their weakest. For the Dog-Star's heat scorches the skin on their bodies, and parches head and feet. At that time let me have a shady rock, and wine of Biblis, a cake of milk-bread, and milk from goats just going dry, and the flesh of a heifer fed in the forest, one that has never calved, or of kids, their mother's first-born. So let me sit in the shade, with a bellyful inside me, comfortably sipping the fire-red wine, and turning to face the breeze from the west.

IV(h) Leaves from a Boeotian farmer's almanack
Hesiod, *Works and Days* 765–89

Mark well and in good order the days that come from Zeus, and explain them to your slaves; that the thirtieth of the month is the best for looking over the work, and dealing out supplies.

And here follow the days that come from Zeus the Counsellor, when men who discern their true nature observe them. First of all, the first, the fourth and the seventh—this last the day on which Leto gave birth to Apollo of the golden blade—are holy days. Then the eighth and the ninth, two days at least of the waxing month, are excellent for the labours of the field. The eleventh day, and the twelfth, too, are both good days either for sheep-shearing or for reaping the good harvest; but of these the twelfth day is far better than the eleventh; for on the twelfth the aerobatic spider spins her web in the full of the day, when Know-all piles up her hill. On this day let the wife set up her loom and get on with her work. In the waxing month the thirteenth is to be avoided for commencing to sow, but for transplanting seedlings it is the best. The sixth of the midmonth is very unfavourable for plants, but good for the birth of boys, but not favourable for girls, either to be born in the first place or to get married. Neither is the first sixth a suitable day for the birth of a girl, but for gelding kids and sheep, and for fencing in a sheep-pen, it is a propitious day. Fine too for a boy to be born; but he will be fond of cutting speech and telling lies, and uttering flattery and smooth talk.

IV(j) Signs of stormy or sunny weather

Aratus, *Weather Signs* 954–88

Cattle, by raising their eyes skywards, get a presentiment of rain from the smell of the atmosphere. Ants hastily remove their eggs from their nests. One sees centipedes climbing *en masse* up walls, and the worms they call the 'entrails of the dark earth' can be seen wandering around. Domestic fowls, the offspring of the cock, peck off their lice vehemently, crowing loudly with a noise like water falling drop by drop. Also the tribe of crows and the race of jackdaws signify the coming of rain from Zeus when they appear in flocks, uttering cries like those of hawks. Crows, when rain is imminent, imitate with their croaking the noise of water coming when, after emitting two deep croaks, they send out a long, strident cry, and flap their wings violently. Domestic ducks, and the jackdaws that live in the eaves, rush towards the gables, flapping their wings, and the heron with a piercing cry sweeps down towards the waves. Do not ignore any of these signs when you wish to take precautions in advance of the rain. Watch out too, if the fleas bite more vigorously than before, and thirst more greedily for your blood, and if the moths, as a storm approaches, gather about the flame of a lamp in a damp evening, and when, with the oncoming storm, the lamplight sometimes burns quite steadily, and sometimes flames leap from it like sparks, or if, in the lamplight itself, rays shine forth; or again if in the cloudless sky of summer the island-dwelling birds fly along in serried ranks. Do not forget either the cauldron or the tripod set on the fire, when it is surrounded by a multitude of sparks, nor when in the glowing embers you see the glitter of metal particles like grains of millet. These are the things to look out for, when watching for the approach of rain.

Fine weather. If from a high mountain-top a vaporous cloud spreads out right down to ground level, and the peaks are shining clear, then you will enjoy fine weather. You will also have fine weather when a low cloud appears on the smooth surface of the sea, and does not lift but lies there heavily like a flat stone. When the weather is fine, look betimes for signs of a storm, and in a storm for signs of a calm. You must also look carefully at the manger from which the Crab moves in its circular path, when it begins to clear itself of all the underlying mist. For she clears herself as the storm is abating. The tranquil flame of lamps and the night-owl with its peaceful song will be a sign that the storm is dying down. Also when at the evening hour the various-sounding rook quickly varies its cry, and when the crows at first singly utter twice over a solitary cry, and afterwards caw loud and shrill with concerted cries; or when they gather in companies when contemplating going to roost, and cry in full voice. One might suppose that they were gladdened by their screeching, and by the sight of themselves around the trees where they roost, or on the tree itself, flapping their wings once more to mark their homecoming. Before a gentle calm the cranes will surely spread their wings, all on the selfsame course; but if they turn back, you will have bad weather.

IV(k) A farmer's almanack

Corpus of Latin Inscriptions v 1.2305 (ILS 8745)

Month of January. 31 days. The Nones fall on the fifth day. The day has 9¾ hours. The night has 14¼ hours. The sun is in the sign of Capricorn. The month is under the protection of Juno. Stakes are sharpened. Willow and reeds are cut. Sacrifices to the household gods.

Month of February. 28 days. The Nones fall on the fifth day. The day has 10¾ hours. The night has 13¼ hours. The sun is in the sign of Aquarius. The month is under the protection of Neptune. The grain fields are weeded. The part of the vines above ground is tended. Reeds are burned. Parentalia, Lupercalia, Dear Relatives' Day, Terminalia.

Month of March. 31 days. The Nones fall on the seventh day. The day has 12 hours. The night has 12 hours. The equinox falls on the twenty-fifth day. The sun is in the sign of Pisces. The month is under the protection of Minerva. The vines are propped up in trenched ground and pruned. Three-month wheat is sown. The bark of Isis. Sacrifices to Mamurius. Liberalia, Quinquatria, Bathing.

Month of April. 30 days. The Nones fall on the fifth day. The day has 13½ hours. The night has 10½ hours. The sun is in the sign of Aries. The month is under the protection of Venus. The lustration of the sheep is made. Sacrifices to the Isis of Pharus. Also festival of Sarapis.

Month of May. 31 days. The Nones fall on the seventh day. The day has 14½ hours. The night has 9½ hours. The sun is in the sign of Taurus. The month is under the protection of Apollo. The grain fields are cleared of weeds. The sheep are shorn. The wool is washed. Young steers are put under the yoke. The vetch for fodder is cut. The lustration of the grain field is made. Sacrifices to Mercury and Flora.

Month of June. 30 days. The Nones fall on the fifth day. The day has 15 hours. The night has 9 hours. The solstice falls on the twenty-fourth day. The sun is in the sign of Gemini. The month is under the protection of Mercury. The hay is mown. The vines are cultivated. Sacrifice to Hercules and Fors Fortuna.

Month of July. 31 days. The Nones fall on the seventh day. The day has 14¼ hours. The night has 9¾ hours. The sun is in the sign of Cancer. The month is under the protection of Jupiter. Barley and beans are harvested. Apollinaria, Neptunalia.

Month of August. 31 days. The Nones fall on the fifth day. The day has 13 hours. The night has 11 hours. The sun is in the sign of Leo. The month is under the protection of Ceres. The stakes are prepared. Cereals are harvested, likewise the wheat. The stubble is burned. Sacrifices to Hope, Safety, and Diana. Volcanalia.

Month of September. 30 days. The Nones fall on the fifth day. The day has 12 hours. The night has 12 hours. The equinox falls on the twenty-fourth day. The sun is in the sign of Virgo. The month is under the protection of Vulcan. The casks are smeared with pitch. Fruits are gathered. The earth around the trees is dug up. Feast of Minerva.

Month of October. 31 days. The Nones fall on the seventh day. The day has 10¾ hours. The night has 13¼ hours. The sun is in the sign of Libra. The month is under the protection of Mars. Grape gathering. Sacrifices to Bacchus.

Month of November. 30 days. The Nones fall on the fifth day. The day has 9½ hours. The night has 14½ hours. The sun is in the sign of Scorpio. The month is under the protection of Diana. Sowing of wheat and barley. Digging of trenches for trees. Feast of Jupiter. Discovery.

Month of December. 31 days. The Nones fall on the fifth day. The day has 9 hours. The night has 15 hours. The sun is in the sign of Sagittarius. The month is under the protection of Vesta. Beginning of winter, or winter solstice. The vines are manured. Beans are sown. Wood is cut. Olives are gathered and also sold. Saturnalia.

IV(l) Spring work on the farm

Virgil, *Georgics* 1.43–70

In early spring, when icy moisture melts on the white mountains,
and crumbling clods loosed to Zephyrus, then is my time for bulls
to start groaning beneath the plough's pressure—for shares,
furrow-rubbed, to gleam. Only *that* sown field answers the
grasping farmer's prayers which twice has felt the sunshine,
twice the cold; its harvests, measureless, have burst the granaries.
But, before tearing open virgin plain with iron, be it our care
to learn the winds, and the sky's various moods, the traditional
tillage and character of places, what every district bears *and*
what it never will. Here crops, there grapes come on more
happily; tree-produce, and grass too, will green unbidden
elsewhere. Do you not see how Tmolus offers saffron perfumes,
India ivory, soft Sabaeans frankincense,
but naked Chalybes iron, Pontus rank castor-oil,
Epirus racing mares to win the palm at Elis?
These laws and treaties Nature has imposed for ever on fixed
localities, right from the time when first into an empty world
Deucalion flung the stones whence humans sprang, a stubborn race.
Therefore press on. Beginning with the year's first months let
mighty bulls turn over the rich soil, and dusty summer days
cook with maturing suns the clods left lying there:
but if the land should not be fertile it suffices hard on
Arcturus' rising to hang the furrow low—
this lest the scanty moisture leaves a sterile sand;
the earlier, lest weeds obstruct the cheerful crops.

GUY LEE

IV(m) Jobs for bad weather and for holidays

Virgil, *Georgics* 1.259–75

If ever the farmer is kept indoors by the cold rain,
much can be done at ease which later would need doing
quickly in clear weather. The ploughman hammers out a blunted
share's hard tooth, hollows boat-troughs from tree-trunks,
brands the cattle or labels all the piles of produce.
Others are sharpening new stakes and two-pronged forks—
preparing Amerian withies to tie the pliant vine.

The bramble canes are woven into baskets now.
Now you must roast the grain, and break it now with stone.
Yes, even on holy days laws human and divine
permit some work to be done. No ordinance forbids
to irrigate the sown field or to fence it off,
make ready snares for birds, burn up the briers and thorns,
and plunge the bleating congregation in healing streams.
Often the donkey-driver loads his slow beast's flanks
with olive oil, or cheap fruit, and on his return
from town brings back a grindstone, or a lump of pitch.

GUY LEE

IV(n) Jobs for night-time and winter

Virgil, *Georgics* 1.287–310

Indeed there's much that's better done in the cool of night
or when at dawn Eous sheds dew on the lands.
At night the light-weight stubble is better mown, at night
dry meadows; for slow moisture never fails the nights.
And there is one who by late fires of winter light
keeps watch and points up torches with a sharpened knife.
Meanwhile to solace with a song the lengthy task
his wife is running the shrill shuttle through the warp
or cooking down the moisture of sweet must with Vulcan
and skimming off with foliage the bubbling cauldron.
But red-cheeked Ceres is cut down in noonday heat
and threshing-floors in noonday heat scour the parched corn.
Plough naked, naked sow. Winter's the tenant's rest.
In the cold weather farmers mostly enjoy their gains,
happily occupied in giving mutual parties.
The genial winter's invitation frees from care,
like as when laden keels have entered port at last
and happy sailors hang their garlands on the stern.
But even so then is the time to gather acorns
and bay-berries and olives and the blood-red myrtle;
time to set snares for game-birds and nets for the stag
and to pursue the long-eared hare; time to shoot deer,
whirling the hempen thongs of a Balearic sling,
when snow lies deep, when rivers hustle ice along.

GUY LEE

IV(o) Meleager's spring song

Palatine Anthology IX.363

Bright spring time smiles with flowery sheen
    Foul winter's winds have flown
Dark earth is clothed in herbage green,
    The leaves, her fresh made gown.
The meadows laugh and drink the dew,
Each morn is bright with roses new.

Now goatherds flute upon the lea,
    And with their younglings play;
Unharmed the ships sail on the sea
    As zephyrs give them way.
With ivy leaves their hair men twine,
And sing the god who gave the vine.

The ox-born bees pursue their toil,
    While with the wax they strive,
And labouring shape the golden spoil
    In myriad chambered hive.
The swan his winter fastness leaves,
The swallow darts among the eaves.

Now woolly sheep together throng
    And in their lambs rejoice;
The wine-god leads the dance and song,
    Earth opens at spring's voice.
The halcyons skim the waves above,
And nightingales fill all the grove.

When trees with tender leaves are gay,
    And sailors sail the seas;
When shepherds pipe a roundelay,
    And swarm the clustering bees;
When every bird is on the wing,
Then how can poets help but sing?

F. A. WRIGHT
(Martial, *Epigrams*, trans. J. A. Pott and
F. A. Wright, London and New York, 1924)

V
SEASONAL OPERATIONS ON THE FARM

It is strange that the only instructions that have come down to us on how to make a plough—by far the most important piece of machinery on the farm—occur in the *Works and Days* and the *Georgics*. Hesiod (Ch. V a) adds specifications for the plough-oxen and some rather naïve hints on how to select a ploughman. The rest of the chapter consists of a representative selection of passages dealing with major operations on the farm. For details of these topics the reader may refer to the relevant sections of my *Roman Farming* (1970). On Varro's contributions here and elsewhere in the book see now the excellent edition of selections by Dr Bertha Tilly, *Varro the Farmer* (1973). The chapter concludes in lighter vein with the young Marcus Aurelius' enthusiastic account of a full and varied day on the farm (Ch. V o).

V(a) On making a plough, and choosing a ploughman

Hesiod, *Works and Days* 427–47

For a waggon ten palms wide, cut a *felloe* * three spans wide. Cut plenty of curved pieces, and carry home a plough-beam of holm-oak, whenever you can find one by looking on the mountain or in the fields. This is the strongest for plough-oxen, when one of Athena's bondsmen has fixed it in the share-beam and fastened it to the pole with dowels. Get ready two ploughs, and work on them at home, one in a single piece, the other jointed; this way is far better, for if you break one of them you can put the oxen to the other. Poles of laurel or elm are the most free of worm; the share-beam should be of oak, and the plough-beam of holm-oak. Get a pair of oxen, nine-year-old males; their strength will be undiminished, since they'll be in their prime, at their best for work. They won't fight in the furrow, and shatter the plough, leaving the work undone. And have a lusty fellow of forty follow them, with a quartered loaf of eight ounces for his dinner, one who'll give his mind to his work, and drive a straight

---

*felloe rim of a wheel.

furrow, and is no longer gawping after his mates, but will keep his thoughts on the job. A younger man will be no better than he at scattering the seeds, and not double-seeding. A younger man hovers around and hankers after his chums.

V(b) On land drainage

Cato, *On Farming* CLV

During the winter the water should be removed from the fields. The drainage ditches on the hillsides must be kept clean. In early autumn, when there is dust about, there is the greatest danger from water. When the rains begin, the whole household must turn out with shovels and hoes, open the ditches, drain off the water on to the roads, and see to it that it runs away. In the farmstead on a rainy day you should make the rounds to see if it is leaking through anywhere, and mark the place with charcoal, so that the tile can be replaced after the rain has stopped. During the growing season wherever water is standing in the growing grain or in the ditches, or if there is any obstruction to the flow of the water, it must be opened and the obstruction removed.

V(c) On ploughing

Pliny, *Natural History* XVIII.177-9

When oxen are going to plough they should be yoked as tightly as possible, to make them keep their heads up when ploughing—this results in a minimum of neck-chafing. If the ploughing is in between trees and vines, they must wear muzzles of soft basketry to prevent them nibbling the most delicate of the buds. A small billhook should be hung on the stilt, for slicing through roots—this is better than tearing them up with the plough, and straining the oxen. When ploughing finish the row, and do not stop to take a breather . . . Every piece of ploughland must be worked with straight furrows, followed by slanting ones. In hilly terrain the plough is only drawn across the slope, but with the share pointing alternately uphill and down; and men have such a capacity for work that they actually perform the function of oxen—at all events mountain people do without this animal, and do their ploughing with the hoe. Unless the plough-man bends to his task he ploughs crooked ('prevaricates')—the charge of pre-varication took its origin from here, and has been transferred to public life: it must always be avoided in the area of its origin. The share should be cleaned from time to time with a stick tipped with a scraper . . . A field that has to be harrowed after the crop has been sown is a badly-ploughed one; a piece of ground will only have been properly tilled if it is impossible to tell which way the share went.

V(d) On hoeing

Columella, *On Farming* II.II.I–IO

Now that we have fully covered the sowing-times for each crop cultivated, we shall indicate the method of cultivation to be used, and the number of man-days of labour needed for each of the crops mentioned. The sowing ended, the next task is that of hoeing, a matter on which authorities disagree. Some say it does no good, since the roots of the grain are exposed by hoeing, and some are even cut off, and if cold weather comes on after the hoeing, the corn is killed by the frost. They hold, on the other hand, that it is more satisfactory for the crop to be weeded and cleaned at the correct season. Still, many approve of hoeing, but say that it should not be done everywhere in the same way and at the same time; in dry and sunny fields, as soon as the plants can stand hoeing, they should be earthed up with well-stirred soil to enable them to bush out; and this should be done before winter, and then done a second time after winter; in cold and swampy places, however, usually after winter is over, they should be hoed without earthing up, but the earth should be well stirred by level hoeing. However, I have discovered that winter hoeing is suited to many regions, but only where the weather is dry and warm enough to allow it, but in my view it should not be universally practised; rather we should conform to local practice. Countries have individual advantages, such as those possessed by Egypt and Africa, where the farmer does not touch his crop between sowing and harvesting: climatic conditions and the quality of the soil are such that scarcely a plant comes up which has not actually been sown; and this is due either to scarcity of rain, or because the condition of the soil shows itself favourable to those who till it. Furthermore, in those areas where hoeing is required, the crops are not to be touched, even if weather conditions allow it, before the growth has covered the furrows. It will be correct to hoe wheat and emmer as soon as they produce four blades, barley when it has five, and beans and the other legumes when they stand four fingers high, with the exception however of the lupine, since hoeing is harmful to its seedlings; it has a single root, and if this is cut or injured by an iron implement, the whole plant dies. Even if this were not the case, cultivation would be superfluous, for this one plant, far from being attacked by weeds, actually kills them of its own accord. Now any other crops which can be disturbed when wet, are nevertheless better hoed when dry; when handled in this way, they are not attacked by rust. Barley, however, must only be touched when perfectly dry. Many people think that beans should not be hoed at all, because, being pulled by hand when ripe, they can be separated from the rest of the growth, and the grass growing among them can be saved for hay. This opinion is also supported by Cornelius Celsus, who also includes this among the other virtues of this legume, when he says that when the beans have been cleared hay may be cut from the same place. In my opinion however it is very poor farming to allow grass to grow up among your crops; if weeding is neglected, there is a heavy reduction in the yield. Nor is it sound husbandry to pay more attention to animal fodder than to human food, especially when you can obtain your fodder by cultivating your pasture. I am so convinced of the necessity of hoeing beans that I believe they should be hoed three times. We find that when cultivated in this way they not only multiply their yield, but they have a much lower percentage of pod; and a measure of them when shelled and cleaned is nearly as full as before shelling, the quantity being hardly reduced by the removal of the pods.

V(e) On manure

Columella, *On Farming* 11.14

The principal kinds of manure are three in number; that from birds, that from humans, and that from cattle. In the category of bird-dung, the best quality is thought to be the dung that is taken from dovecotes; next, that which comes from hens and other birds, with the exception however of marsh fowl or birds that swim, such as ducks and geese; for this is positively harmful. We strongly recommend pigeon dung, because we find that a moderate scattering causes the earth to ferment; in second place comes human dung, if mixed with other farm-yard refuse: it is naturally rather hot, and for that reason burns the earth. More suited to young shoots is human urine; if allowed to mature for six months and then applied to vines or fruit trees, it is better than anything else for increasing the yield of fruit. In addition to producing a large crop, this treatment also improves the flavour and the bouquet of the wine and the fruit. Also old oil-lees, unsalted and mixed with this, can be used to good effect in watering fruit trees and especially olives; the lees too is very beneficial even when applied neat. But both are used mainly during winter, and even in springtime before the summer heat, while the ground is opened up around the vines and the trees. Cattle-dung holds third place, and in this category too there is a difference, dung produced by donkeys is regarded as the best, because the animal chews very slowly and hence digests its food more readily, and yields a manure that is well made and suitable for immediate application. After the above-mentioned kinds comes sheep dung, followed by goat dung, and then that of other cattle and draught animals. Pig-manure is considered the poorest of all. In addition, the use of ashes and cinders is quite useful, while lupine plants when cut down have the strength of the best manure. I am well aware that there is a type of countryside in which neither cattle nor fowl can be kept; but even in a place like this it is a sign of lazy farming to be short of fertilizer. You can gather up any sort of leaves; any accumulated matter from brier patches and from high-ways and byways; you may cut down your neighbour's bracken without doing him any harm, or even as a favour, and mix it with the sweepings from the yard;

you may dig a trench like the one I gave instructions for making in my first book for storing manure, and may pile together in a single heap ashes, sewer sludge, straw, and whatever else is swept out. But it is a good idea to plant a piece of oak wood in the centre of the place; this prevents the noxious snake from hiding in the dung.

V(f) On harvesting, threshing and winnowing of grain

Columella, *On Farming* 11.20

But when the corn is ripe, it should be quickly harvested, before it can get parched by the heat of the summer sun, which is most devastating during the rising of the Dog-star; delay is expensive, in the first place because it offers plunder to birds and other creatures, and secondly, because the grains and even the heads themselves drop off quickly as the stalks and beards wither. Indeed, if windstorms or cyclones assail it, the greater part of it sinks to the ground; this is why there must be no delay, but when the crop is an even golden colour, before the grains have completely hardened, and after they have attained a reddish colour the crop must be harvested, so that the grain may swell on the threshing-floor, and in the stack and not in the field. For it is agreed that, if cut at the correct time, it subsequently makes some growth. There are, however, numerous methods of reaping. Many cut the straw in the middle with spitted scythes (these are either bill-shaped or toothed); many gather the heads only with reaping-boards and others with combs—a method which is very easy in a thin crop, but extremely difficult in a dense one.

But if the grain, with part of the stalk, is cut with sickles, it is immediately gathered into a stack, or carried into the drying shed, and then, being exposed to sunshine from time to time, as opportunity offers, it is threshed. However, if the heads alone are cut off, they can be brought into the granary, and then, during winter, be either beaten out with flails or trodden out by cattle. But if it is possible to have the corn threshed on the floor, there is no doubt that this job is better done with horses than with oxen, and if you haven't many teams, you can hitch them to a threshing-sledge or a drag; either of these implements very easily breaks up the straw. It is better, however, for the heads themselves to be beaten with flails and cleaned in winnowing baskets. But when the grains are mixed with chaff, they are separated by the wind. The west wind is regarded as excellent for this purpose, since it blows light and steady during the summer months. But to wait for it betrays the dilatory farmer, for often while we are waiting, we are taken by surprise by a violent storm. Hence the threshed grain should be piled up on the threshing-floor in such a way that it can be winnowed with any breath of wind. If, however, there is a total lack of breeze in all quarters over many days, the grain should be cleaned with winnowing baskets, in case a destructive storm following extreme inactivity on the part of the winds may nullify the efforts of an entire year. Then the clean grain, if it is to be stored away for a period of years, should be threshed again, for the cleaner it is the less it is eaten away by weevils; if on the other hand, it is marked down for immediate use, a second cleaning is pointless, and it is sufficient for it to be cooled in the shade and so brought into the barn. The treatment of legumes too is in no way different from that of other grains; they too are either consumed straight away or stored. And this is the crowning reward of the husbandman, to reap the harvest of the seeds he has committed to the ground.

V(g) The threshing-floor

Varro, *On Farming* 1.51

The threshing-floor should be on the farmland, on somewhat elevated ground, so that the wind can blow through it; it should be of moderate size, and proportioned to the size of the crop, round for choice, with a slight protuberance at the centre, so that, if it rains, the water may not stand, but be able to run off outside the threshing-floor by the shortest possible route, and in a circle the shortest lines are those from the centre to the circumference. It should be of solid earth well rammed, especially if it is of clay, so that it may not be cracked by the heat, allowing the grains to get lost in the cracks, or take in water, and make openings for mice and ants. To stop this it is usual to drench it with oil-dregs, which are poison to weeds, ants and moles. Some farmers build up the floor with stone, to give it a solid surface, or even pave it. Others, such as the Bagienni, even roof their threshing-floors, because in their country storms are very prevalent at harvest time. When the floor is without a roof and the climate is hot, a shelter should be constructed near by, to which the workers may go in the heat of midday.

The largest and finest crop should be taken separately to the threshing-floor, and the ears threshed separately, so that the farmer may have the best possible seed-corn. The grains should be threshed out of the ears on the floor. Some farmers do this by means of yoked oxen and a threshing-sledge, which is made either from a plank roughened by stones or iron spikes, on which the driver stands or a large weight is placed; the implement is then dragged by the yoke of draught animals, and shakes the grains out of the ears. Or it is made of toothed axles equipped with small wheels, and is called a Punic cart; someone has to sit on it and drive the animals which pull it, as is the practice in Hither Spain and elsewhere. Among other peoples the threshing is done by driving in a herd of cattle, and keeping them on the move with poles, the grain being rubbed out of the ears by their hoofs. After the threshing the grain should be tossed up in the air, when a gentle breeze is blowing, with winnowing forks or shovels. This causes the lightest portion of it, called chaff, to be blown away outside the threshing-floor, while the heavy portion, the grain, comes clean to the basket.

When the harvest is finished the gleaning should be put up for sale, or the loose stalks gathered with your own labour force; or else, if the ears are few and the cost of labour high, it should be eaten down. The important thing to be kept in view in this exercise is to prevent the cost exceeding the profit.

V(h) On haymaking

Pliny, *Natural History* XVIII.260-1

Some farmers irrigate the day before they mow, but where there are no irrigation ditches, it is better to mow after nights of heavy dew. In some parts of Italy they mow after the harvest. Mowing was also a more expensive operation in earlier days, when only Cretan and other imported whetstones were known, and these only used oil to put an edge on the blade. Consequently a man making hay would walk along with a horn to hold the oil tied to his leg. Italy gave us whetstones that employ water, which are used to keep the steel in order instead of a file, but the water very quickly makes them grow green with rust. There are two types of scythe; the Italian variety is shorter, and easy to use even among brambles, while those used on the Gallic latifundia are bigger; in fact they economize by cutting through the stalks at middle height, and missing out the shorter ones. Italian mowers use only the right hand in cutting.

V(j) How to train vines

Pliny, *Natural History* XVII.164-6

The management of the nursery is followed by the arrangement of vineyards. There are five types: (1) with the shoots spread over the ground: (2) with self-supporting vines: (3) with a prop but no cross-bar: (4) with the vine propped by a single cross-bar: (5) trellised with a rectangular frame. It will be understood that the propped-vine method and that of the unpropped, free-standing vine, belong to one and the same system: the latter method is only used where there is a shortage of props. Vines with the single prop are extended in straight rows, this form being called a gelding (*canterius*). This is better for wine-grapes, since the vine does not get in its own shadow, is ripened by continuous sunshine, and is more affected by air flow, and so gets rid of dew more rapidly; also it makes trimming and harrowing and all other operations easier. Above all, it sheds its blossoms in a more beneficial way. The cross-bar is formed by a stake or a reed, or else of a rope made from hair or hemp, as in Spain and at Brindisi. The rectangular frame type of vine produces more wine (it takes its name from the rectangular openings in the roofs of our houses); the trellis is divided into four compartments by the same number of cross-pieces.

V(k) The vintage

Varro, *On Farming* 1.54

In the vineyards you must get on with the vintage when the grapes are ripe, although you should make up your mind first on the variety of grape and the section of vineyard with which you intend to begin. The early grapes, and the common hybrid, which they call black, ripen much earlier (than the rest) and for that reason must be picked first; and the sunnier section of the plantation and the vineyard ought to be stripped first. During the vintage the careful farmer not only gathers, but selects his clusters; he gathers for drinking, and selects for eating. Consequently, those that are gathered are taken to the vineyard to go from there into the empty storage jar; those selected are placed in a separate basket to be transferred into small jars, and then thrust into large storage jars full of grape refuse; others to be let down in a pitch-coated jar into the pond, while others still go up to a place in the larder. The stalks and skins of grapes that have been trodden must be placed under the press, so that any must remaining in them may be squeezed out into the same vat. Some people, when the juice stops flowing under the press, trim round the edges of the mass, and press again; the juice from the second pressing, known as *circumsicium*, is kept separate, because it tastes of iron. The pressed grape-skins are thrown into casks, and water is added; this liquid is called *lora*, an abbreviation for *lora acina**, and is given to the labourers in winter instead of wine.

V(l) On treading the grapes

Geoponics VI.II

Those who are in charge of the larger baskets called panniers must pick out the leaves and any sour grapes or wizened clusters. Those who tread must pick out anything that has been missed out by those in charge of the baskets; for the leaves, if pressed with the grapes, render the wine rougher and more apt to spoil; and great damage is caused by grapes that are dry or sour. Those who are charged with this task must immediately press with their feet the grapes that are thrown into the vats, and having equally trodden all the grape-stones, they must pick up the kernels, that is, the refuse, so that most of the liquor may run

---

*lora acina watered grape-skins.

into the channel. . . . The men that tread must get into the press, having scrupulously cleaned their feet, and none of them must eat or drink while in the press, nor must they climb in and out frequently. If they have to leave the press, they must not go with bare feet. The men that tread must also be fully clad and have their girdles on, on account of the violent sweating. It is also proper to have the presses fumigated, either with frankincense or with some other sweet odour.

V(m) On gathering and processing olives
Varro, On Farming 1.55

We come now to the olive plantation. Olives that can be reached from the ground or from ladders should be picked rather than shaken down, because fruit that has been struck loses flesh and yields less oil. Those that are picked by hand are better gathered with the bare fingers, not with pincers [gloves?] for the hardness of the latter bruises not only the berry but the bark of the branches and leaves them exposed to frost. Those that are out of reach should be beaten down, but with a reed rather than a pole, as the heavier blow calls in the services of the doctor. The beater should not strike the fruit directly; an olive struck in this way often carries away with it a green shoot from the branch, and next year's fruit is lost, and this is among the strongest reasons for the saying that the olive fails to bear fruits every other year, or bears a reduced crop. The olive reaches the farmstead by the same two routes as the grape, some for eating, others to be liquified and anoint the body both within and without, thus following the master to the baths and the gymnasium. The second class of olives, from which oil is made, are usually piled up in heaps (one heap for each day) on shelves, there to become moderately soft; when they are made to pass down, in the order in which they were laid, through the jars and pans to the trapetae, a device consisting of millstones of hard and rough stone used for crushing the olives. Olives which remain too long in the heaps after picking go soft from the heat, and the oil goes rancid; hence if you are unable to make your oil in good time you must air them by moving them about in the piles. The olive yields two products: (1) the oil, which everyone knows about and (2) amurca*. As most people are ignorant of the value of amurca, you may see it running from the oil-presses into the fields, and not only blackening the earth, but, when there is a large quantity of it, making it barren. In fact this liquid, when used in moderation, is of the greatest importance in farming, as well as for many other purposes. It is commonly poured round the roots of trees, especially olives, and wherever there are noxious weeds in the ground.

---

*amurca a watery scum left after the pressing.

V(n) Contracts for harvesting grapes and for the sale of grapes and wine

Cato, *On Farming* CXLIV–CXLVIII

The olive harvest should be put out to contract in the following manner: The contractor shall gather the whole olive crop correctly according to the wishes of the owner or the overseer whom he has appointed or the buyer to whom the olive crop has been sold. He shall not pick the olives nor beat them down without an order from the owner or his representative. If anyone violates this rule, no one shall pay for what he has gathered on that day, and no payment will be owing.

All gatherers will swear in the presence of the owner or the overseer that they have not stolen olives, nor has anyone with their connivance stolen any from the estate of L. Manlius during that harvest. If any of them refuses to take this oath, no one shall pay for what he has gathered, and no payment shall be due to him. The contractor shall give security to the satisfaction of L. Manlius for the olives to be properly gathered. Ladders are to be returned in the same condition in which they were issued, except if some old ones have been broken. If they are not returned, a fair deduction shall be made according to the decision of an honest man. Any damage done to the owner through the fault of the contractor will be made good by him, the deduction to be made according to the decision of an honest man . . . No contractor shall go off to where the gathering and pressing of the olives is being farmed out at a higher price except when he has nominated a substitute for the present contract. If anyone violates this rule, if the owner or the overseer desire it all the partners shall swear an oath. If they fail to do so, no one shall pay for gathering and pressing the olives, and nothing will be owing to one who has not so sworn. Bonuses: For every 1200 *modii**, there is an allowance of five *modii* of salted olives, nine pounds of pure oil, and five amphorae of vinegar for the whole harvest. For the portion of salted olives they do not receive during the harvest they shall be given five sesterces for each lot of five *modii*.

Conditions for the sale of grapes on the vine: The buyer shall leave the grape-skins without wetting them, and the lees. Storage room for the wine shall be given up to the Kalends of October following. If he does not remove it before that the owner shall do what he likes with the wine. All other conditions are the same as those applied to olives on the trees.

Conditions for the sale of wine in jars: For every *culleus*† of wine sold, forty-one half-amphorae shall be delivered, and only wine that is neither sour nor musty will be delivered. Within two days thereafter it shall be tasted to the

---

*modius dry measure = *c.* 1 bushel.
†See p.29.n.

satisfaction of a good man. If the buyer neglects to do this, it shall be regarded as tasted. Days during which the tasting was delayed through the owner's fault shall be counted to the benefit of the buyer. The buyer shall take over the wine before the Kalends of January following. If he fails to do so, the owner will measure the wine, and the buyer will pay for it as measured by the owner. If the buyer asks for it, the owner will swear that he has measured it honestly. Storage will be permitted up to the Kalends of October following. If the buyer does not take it away before that the owner shall do what he likes with it. The rest of the law is the same as that for olives on the tree.

V(o) A day on an imperial farm

Fronto, *Letters* iv.6 (from Marcus Aurelius to his Tutor, Fronto)

Hello, my dearest teacher.
We are well. I slept-in a little because of my cold, which seems to be better now. I occupied my time from the 11th hour of the night to the 3rd hour of the day reading Cato's book called 'Agriculture' and doing some writing—not such appalling rubbish as yesterday! Then I went to say good morning to my father. I treated my sore throat by swallowing some honey and water into the back of my throat and spitting it out again. (I don't want to say 'gargle'—it's not a good word.) After that I went and stood beside my father at a sacrifice. Then we went to lunch. Guess what I ate! A tiny bit of bread—though I could see the others wolfing down beans and onions and herrings full of roe. Next we worked hard at picking grapes till we were covered with sweat and shouting with merriment. (We didn't forget to leave some bunches hanging up high as the poet tells us to do.) Then, at the end of the 6th hour, we made our way home. I did a little studying, but it was no good. Then I had a long chat with my little mother sitting on the bed. I said, 'What do you think my Fronto is doing right now?' and she said, 'What do you think my Gratia is doing?' and so on. While we were chatting away the gong went to tell us that father had gone for his bath. We had supper after our bath in the room which has the oil presses. I don't mean we had a bath in the oil-press room! I mean we had our supper there after our bath! We enjoyed listening to the farm hands cracking jokes about each other. Then I went off to bed, but before rolling over and starting to snore I did my duty and wrote a complete account of the day's happenings for my dearest teacher.

Good-bye, Fronto,
Wherever you are.

VI
OUT ON THE RANGE

The contents of this chapter are by no means covered by the title: animal husbandry in classical times included the breeding, training and care of the all-important plough-oxen, as well as the donkeys and mules that provided the motive power for many other tasks around the farm, and for the movement of goods by road. Sheep were also kept on the mixed farm to provide clothing, food and manure for the soil. The ranching or range-farming which came to dominate a great part of southern Italy during the late Republic and early Empire involved a two-way seasonal movement of sheep and cattle between coastal flats and upland pastures over well-worn trails. All these aspects, and many more, are discussed at length by the Roman agronomists, and our selection is no more than an introduction to a vast subject.

Varro's account of the shepherds out on the range (Ch. VI a) is of outstanding interest, bringing out the hardships imposed by this sort of existence, as well as the qualities of vigour and endurance that it demands, both from the shepherds and from their womenfolk. At Ch. VI(e) Virgil describes the hardships of herdsmen in two distant regions in sharply contrasted climates—those of the nomads of north Africa and those of the cattlemen of the icy Scythian steppes. Selections from the agronomists give details of the management, training and rearing of farm animals (Ch. VI f, g, h). Ch. VI(j) forms part of a lengthy account, given in a public lecture by Dio Chrysostom, purporting to reflect the run-down state of the land in the once prosperous Greek island of Euboea. Whatever may have been the writer's own contribution to the story of these hard-working and resourceful squatters, there is nothing outrageously improbable in the account. Ch. VI(d) and VI(k) illustrate some of the problems arising from the presence of animals in transit on the roads. Real shepherds, as distinct from their literary counterparts, had nothing to sing about; when the victims of Marcus Aurelius' piece of royal horseplay 'had at last rounded up their flock and put their courage away for the next and perhaps more serious encounter with real brigands, they could exchange a hundred true tales of raids, robberies and rustling' (Ramsay MacMullen, *Roman Social Relations*, 1974—in a chapter full of pertinent references).

VI(a) The shepherds and their life on the range

Varro, *On Farming* II.10

Atticus looked round to see if he had overlooked any point, and I remarked:
'This silence provides a cue for another actor to come on stage; for the remaining scene in this act is to discover the number and types of herdsmen to be kept.'
Thereupon Cossinius observed: 'For the larger cattle you will need older men,
for the smaller even boys will do, but those, whether men or boys, who pass
their lives out on the trails must be sturdier than those who return home to the
farmstead every day. Thus on the range you may see men in their prime, and
usually armed, while on the home farm, not only boys but even girls look after
the flocks. The herdsmen are obliged to stay out on the range all day long, and
have their herds graze together, but they must spend the night each with his
own herd, and all should be under a single flockmaster. He should preferably
be older than the others, and also more experienced, since the others will be
more favourably disposed to take orders from a man who is their superior both
in years and in knowledge. Still, he mustn't be so much older that he is incapable,
through senility, of standing up to hard work. In fact, the very old and the very
young find it difficult to endure the hardships of the trail, and the steepness and
ruggedness of the mountains; and such hardships are inevitable for those who
follow the herd, especially herds of cattle and goats, which love to feed in rocky,
wooded country. The type of man selected for this work should be strong, swift,
agile and supple of limb; men who, as well as following the flock, can also defend
it against wild beasts and robbers; men able to lift loads on to the backs of pack-
animals, to dash out ahead, and to hurl javelins . . . In the daytime the shepherds
of each separate flock should eat by themselves, but in the evening all those who
are under one head shepherd should eat together. The head shepherd should see
that all the equipment needed for the animals and the shepherds goes with
them, especially what is needed for the sustenance of the men and the medical
care of the animals. For this purpose some owners keep pack-animals, others
mares, while some, instead of the above, keep some other animal capable of
carrying loads on its back.

'As to the breeding of the men, there is no problem in the case of the shepherd
who stays permanently on the farm, since he has a female fellow-slave on the
farmstead, and the Venus of herdsmen looks no further than this. But as for
those who pasture their flocks in mountain glens and wooded regions, finding
shelter from storms not in a farmhouse, but in makeshift huts, many owners
have thought it advisable to have them accompanied by women, who can
follow the flocks, prepare the shepherds' meals, and make the men more atten-
tive to their work. These women should however be able-bodied, and not bad-
looking. In many areas they are as good workers as the men—a fact you may
notice everywhere in Illyricum, where they can either do the shepherding, or

bring logs for the fire and cook the food, or look after the farm implements in the huts. As for the feeding of the young, I may just mention that in most cases the mothers suckle their own babies.' At the same time he looked at me and declared: 'I've heard you say that when you went to Croatia you saw mothers carrying logs and at the same time children whom they were suckling, sometimes one, sometimes two; thus proving that our newly delivered women who lie for days under mosquito nets are feeble and contemptible.' 'Quite true,' I replied; 'and in Illyricum I have seen an even more cogent illustration; there pregnant women, when the time for delivery has arrived, often withdraw a short distance from where they are working, give birth there, and come back with the child you would think they had found, not borne. Another very striking fact is that women in that country, known as "maidens", even at the age of twenty, are not forbidden by local custom to sleep with anybody they like before marriage, to wander about by themselves, and to produce children.'

VI(b) Battle for leadership of the herd

Virgil, *Georgics* III. 209–41

But no device so fortifies their power
As love's blind stings of passion to forefend,
Whether on steed or steer thy choice be set.
Ay, therefore 'tis they banish bulls afar
To solitary pastures, or behind
Some mountain-barrier, or broad streams beyond,
Or else in plenteous stalls pen fast at home.
For even through sight of her, the female wastes
His strength with smouldering fire, till he forget
Both grass and woodland. She indeed full oft
With her sweet charms can lovers proud compel
To battle for the conquest horn to horn.
In Sila's forest feeds the heifer fair,
While each on each the furious rivals run:
Wound follows wound; the black blood laves their limbs;
Horns push and strive against opposing horns,
With mighty groaning; all the forest-side
And far Olympus bellow back the roar.
Nor wont the champions in one stall to couch;
But he that's worsted hies him to strange climes
Far off, an exile, moaning much the shame,
The blows of that proud conqueror, then love's loss
Avenged not; with one glance toward the byre,
His ancient royalties behind him lie.

1. Goatherd resting near rural sanctuary; detail from a 'sacro-idyllic' mural painting from the Villa of Agrippa Postumus at Boscotrecase. Naples: National Museum.

2. *opposite top* Reconstruction of a Roman *villa rustica* at Boscoreale, near Pompeii, showing courtyard with buried fermentation jars (*dolia*), press rooms for grapes and olives, and domestic buildings. Rome: Museum of Roman Civilization.

3. *opposite bottom* Reconstruction of a large Romano-British farm complex at Lullingstone, Kent, showing in the grounds a domed temple and a mausoleum. Second to fourth century A.D. Drawn by Alan Sorrell.

4. *above* Rocky North African landscape with vines and olives, farm workers, huntsmen and hounds. Upper register, a stream of water issues from a water-tower into a sluice for irrigation; lower register to l., a door leading to a bath-house?, to r., a birdcatcher approaching a tree.

5. Pastoral scene, with architectural 'folly', set against a mountainous backdrop. Wall painting from Pompeii; before A.D. 79. Naples: National Museum.

6. River landscape with 'pack-horse' bridge, cattle, cowherds, and a traveller with knapsack and stick. Mural painting from a villa on the Appian Way, near Rome. Second century A.D. Rome: Villa Albani.

7. Shepherd and his flock. Wall painting (detail) from the *columbarium* of the Villa Pamphili, Rome. Last quarter of the first century B.C. Rome: National Museum.

8. *below* Light four-wheeled passenger vehicle drawn by a pair of mules. Mosaic in Ostia. Third century A.D.

9. *bottom* Four-wheeled cart, containing hunting equipment, and covered with netting; to r., a birdcatcher. Mosaic from Orbe, Switzerland.

10. *opposite top* country residence at Tabarka, near Tunis, comprising walled courtyard, pillared portico, and massive corner towers. Livestock includes pheasants, geese and ducks. Mosaic lunette. Tunis: Bardo Museum.

11. *opposite bottom* The hunt sets off; in background, villa with altar. Floor mosaic (detail) from Henchir Toungar, Tunisia. Tunis, Bardo Museum.

(a)

(c)

12. Four of the panels representing seasonal activities on the farm, from Vienne, France: (a) basket-maker at work, showing crate-rods and osiers; another worker brings fresh supplies of willow; (b) cleaning and pitching storage jars in preparation for the vintage; (c) treading the grapes; (d) pressing grapes in the lever-press; note the press-man leaning out to obtain better leverage.

13. Four further panels from Vienne: (a) offerings to a woodland god (Faunus? Silvanus?) at a rustic shrine; (b) picking olives; (c) sowing beans? in rows; (d) ploughing in an orchard. Gallo-Roman floor mosaic. Saint-Germain-en-Laye: National Museum of Antiquities of France

14. *above* The harvest-home. Procession of harvesters returning from the field, led by a sistrum-player and a choir (top). Vase of black steatite from Hagia Triada, Crete. 1550–1500 B.C. Heraklion Museum.

15. *opposite* Herdsman watching his flock, with a pair of dogs beside him. Attic black-figured drinking cup (*kyathos*). Sixth century B.C. Paris: Louvre.

16. *above* Labourers in cowled tunics working in the fields at the entrance to a large Gallo-Roman farm. Wall painting from Trier, W. Germany. Second to third century A.D. Trier: Landesmuseum.

17. *below* Gallo-Roman funerary relief, depicting (top centre) the funeral repast, bottom centre., the farmer returning from haymaking. From the hill-top stronghold (*oppidum*) of Montauban-Buzenol, S. Belgium.

18. *opposite top* Threshing corn with cattle and horses; large farmstead in background. Floor mosaic from Dar Buc Ammera, near Zliten, Tripolitania. *c.* 300 A.D. Tripoli: Archaeological Museum. Photo: Roger Wood, London.

19. *opposite bottom* Life on a North African estate. The scenes include (centre back) a ploughman loosing his oxen as other animals make for the stalls; a horse drinking at a trough fed by a swipe; to r. a shepherd pipes to his flock while another does the milking; beyond them a worker knocks down olives with canes. The hunting scenes (l. and centre front) include a boar-hunt and a decoy-lure for partridges. Floor mosaic from Oudna, near Carthage. Tunis: Bardo Museum.

20. *opposite top* Going to market; farmer, laden with produce, arriving at the town gate. Above l., shrine of Priapus; above centre, sanctuary of Bacchus, with mystical winnowing basket. Munich.

21. *opposite bottom* A country siesta; above, centre, a naked cowherd reclines exhausted beside a tree, on which he has hung his tunic. To his r., a Priapus figure before an altar; to his l., his dog prowls on watch, while below his herd rests in the shade. Munich.

22. *top* Ceremony of the Piglambull (*Souvetaurilia*) in honour of Mars. Procession to the altar, where the veiled priest, preparing to sacrifice, scatters incense from a box held open for him. Paris: Louvre.

23. *above* Out on the pastures. Herdsman with horses, cattle, sheep and goats; lower l., a shepherd milking a ewe; upper l., another cuts leaves for fodder, while a third (bottom r.), watches his grazing flock. Relief from sarcophagus. Third century A.D. Rome: National Museum.

24. Pastoral scene with cattle, sheep, cowherds and shepherds. Illustrated page from a manuscript of Virgil, illustrating the Third Georgic. Codex Romanus (*Vat. lat.* no. 3867), fifth century A.D. Vatican Library.

25. A shepherd with his goats. Silver dish, from Klimova, USSR. Middle of sixth century A.D. Leningrad: Hermitage Museum.

26. *opposite top* Slave carrying a hare. Detail from the great Vine mosaic, Cherchel, Algeria. Cherchel Museum.

27. *opposite bottom* Man butchering pig. From the great Vine mosaic, Cherchel, Algeria. Cherchel Museum.

28. *above* Going to market; l., the customer; r., the pig-seller, who has other goods for sale in his shoulder panniers. Attic red-figured vase *c.* 460 B.C. Cambridge: Fitzwilliam Museum.

(a)

(b)

(c)

29. *above* Hunting scenes from the Royal Hunting Lodge, Piazza Armerina, Sicily. Details from the Hunt Corridor mosaic: (a) sacrifice before the hunt; (b) killing a hare in its form; (c) bringing home the wild boar. Mid fourth century A.D.

30. *opposite top* Fishing scenes from an Etruscan tomb. As wild ducks fly overhead, a fisherman sinks his lines, while another hauls in his catch as dolphins leap around the vessel's bows. Part of a wall painting of the sixth century B.C. Tarquinia, Tomba della Caccia e della Pesce.

31. *opposite bottom* Capturing wild animals for shipment to the Games. African beaters are shown closing in on the beasts as they manoeuvre them into the transport cages, which were baited with meat. Mosaic in Anaaba Museum, Algeria. Photo: Roger Wood, London.

32. *opposite* Fresco painting from Stabiae, near Pompeii, depicting Flora, goddess of spring and of flowers; sometimes given the title of *La Primavera*. Naples: National Museum.

33. *above* Scenes from a Spanish health resort. Silver cup adorned with reliefs; top, Health (*Salus*) personified, reclining, her l. hand leaning on an urn from which a stream flows into a tank (a local medicinal spring). Other figures include an old man 'taking the waters', a recovered patient sacrificing, and a mule-cart conveying spa water for export? Madrid: National Museum.

34. The Four Seasons, from the Seasons mosaic, Vienne: (a) Spring, (b) Summer, (c) Autumn, (d) Winter. Saint-Germain-en-Laye: National Museum of Antiquities of France.

So with all heed his strength he practiseth,
And nightlong makes the hard bare stones his bed,
And feeds on prickly leaf and pointed rush,
And proves himself, and butting at a tree
Learns to fling wrath into his horns, with blows
Provokes the air, and scattering clouds of sand
Makes prelude of the battle; afterward,
With strength repaired and gathered might breaks camp,
And hurls him headlong on the unthinking foe:
As in mid ocean when a wave far off
Begins to whiten, mustering from the main
Its rounded breast, and, onward rolled to land
Falls with prodigious roar among the rocks,
Huge as a very mountain: but the depths
Upseethe in swirling eddies, and disgorge
The murky sand-lees from their sunken bed.

JAMES RHOADES
(Virgil, *The Georgics*, trans. James Rhoades,
London, 1881)

VI(c) On sheep-shearing
Varro, *On Farming* II.11.6–9

As for sheep-shearing, I first take careful notice, before starting the work, to see whether the sheep are suffering from scab or sores, so that they may be treated, if necessary, before shearing. The proper time for shearing is between the vernal equinox and the summer solstice, after the sheep have begun to sweat. It is from this sweat (*sudor*) that freshly shorn wool gets its name of 'juicy' (*sucida*). Newly shorn sheep are rubbed down on the same day with wine and oil, but some people add a mixture of white wax and bacon fat; if they are used to wearing a jacket, they completely grease on the inside with the same mixture the skin with which they were covered, and put it on again. If a sheep is nicked during the shearing, they smear the wound with liquid pitch. Coarse-woolled sheep are shorn here about the time of the barley harvest, elsewhere before the cutting of the hay. Some farmers shear their sheep twice a year—as is the case in Hither Spain—that is, every six months, putting in double work with the idea of getting more wool—a motive that induces some to mow their meadows twice a year. The more careful farmers spread little mats under the sheep, and shear the sheep over them, to avoid losing any flocks. Cloudless days are chosen for this job, which usually goes on from 10 a.m. to 4 p.m. The fleece from a sheep that is sheared in hot sunshine gains in softness from the sweat, as well as in weight, and has a better colour. This wool, when removed and heaped

77

together is called by some *vellera*, by others *vellimna*. From this word it may be inferred that in wool-making plucking was discovered before shearing. Even today some people pluck out the wool, and they deprive the sheep of food for three days beforehand, since they hold the roots of the wool less tightly when weak.

VI(d) Trouble on a cattle ranch

Corpus of Latin Inscriptions I X.2438, A.D. 169/72

'Letter written by Cosmus, freedman of the emperor and financial secretary, to Bassaeus Rufus and Macrinius Vindex, Prefects of the Praetorian Guard, men of the highest rank. I have appended a copy of a letter written to me by Septimianus, my fellow-freedman and assistant, and I request you kindly to write to the magistrates of Saepinum and Bovianum, instructing them not to abuse the renters of the flocks of sheep, who are under my control, so that through your good offices the imperial treasury may be protected against loss.' 'Letter written by Septimianus to Cosmus. Since the renters of the flocks of sheep, who are under your control, are now repeatedly complaining to me that they are frequently ill-treated by the imperial police and the authorities at Saepinum and Bovianum, on the mountain cattle-trails, in that they detain in transit draught animals and shepherds hired by them, declaring that they are runaway slaves and have stolen the animals—and on this pretext even sheep belonging to the emperor go missing during these disturbances—we deemed it necessary to write to them again and again, warning them to behave with more moderation, to prevent loss to imperial property.'

VI(e) Animal husbandry in Africa and Scythia

Virgil, Georgics III.339–70

Of Libya's shepherds why the tale pursue?
Why sing their pastures and the scattered huts
They house in? Oft their cattle day and night
Graze the whole month together, and go forth
Into far deserts where no shelter is,
So flat the plain and boundless. All his goods
The Afric swain bears with him, house and home,
Arms, Cretan quiver, and Amyclaean dog;
As some keen Roman in his country's arms
Plies the swift march beneath a cruel load;
Soon with tents pitched and at his post he stands,
Ere looked for by the foe. Not thus the tribes

Of Scythia by the far Maeotic wave,
Where turbid Ister whirls his yellow sands,
And Rhodope stretched out beneath the pole
Comes trending backward. There the herds they keep
Close-pent in byres, nor any grass is seen
Upon the plain, nor leaves upon the tree:
But with snow-ridges and deep frost afar
Heaped seven ells high the earth lies featureless:
Still winter! still the north wind's icy breath!
Nay, never sun disparts the shadows pale,
Or as he rides the steep of heaven, or dips
In ocean's fiery bath his plunging car.
Quick ice-crusts curdle on the running stream,
And iron-hooped wheels the water's back now bears,
To broad wains opened, as erewhile to ships;
Brass vessels oft asunder burst, and clothes
Stiffen upon the wearers; juicy wines
They cleave with axe; to one frozen mass
Whole pools are turned; and on their untrimmed beards
Stiff clings the jagged icicle. Meanwhile
All heaven no less is filled with falling snow;
The cattle perish: oxen's mighty frames
Stand island-like amid the frost, and stags
In huddling herds, by that strange weight benumbed,
Scarce top the surface with their antler-points.

JAMES RHOADES
(Virgil, *The Georgics*, trans. James Rhoades,
London, 1881)

VI(f) On flock management

Columella, *On Farming* VII.3.23–6

But around the rising of the Dog-star we must pay attention to the summer weather conditions, so that before midday the flock is driven westwards and advances in that direction, but after midday it is driven eastwards, since it is of the greatest importance not to let their heads as they graze face into the sun, which is generally harmful to animals at the rising of the above-mentioned constellation. In winter and spring they should be kept in their enclosures during the morning hours, until the sun removes the hoar-frost from the fields; for frost-covered grass promotes catarrh in cattle and loosens the bowels. That is why it is also necessary in the cool and wet seasons of the year to allow them water only once a day.

The man who follows the flock should be observant and alert (these qualifications apply to anyone put in charge of any four-footed animal), and should be very gentle in his control of them; he should also keep close to them, and, when driving them out or bringing them home, he should threaten them by shouting at them or with his crook; but never throw a missile at them; he should not withdraw too far from them, nor should he lie down or sit down; unless he is moving forward he should stand upright, for the job of a shepherd calls for a lofty and commanding look-out point, so that he can prevent the slower pregnant ewes, as they move sluggishly, and the more active ones, who have already dropped their lambs, as they push ahead, from getting cut off from the rest of the flock, in case a thief or a wild beast may trap the shepherd while daydreaming.

VI(g) How to train oxen to the plough

Columella, On Farming VI.2

If however the steers are mild-tempered and quiet, you will be able to drive them out even on the day on which you have tethered them, and before nightfall, training them to walk a thousand paces in good order and without showing fear. When you have led them home again, you must tie them tightly to the posts, in such a way that they cannot move their heads. Then is the time to approach the oxen, when they are tied up, not from behind or from the flanks, but head on, quietly, and with a soothing tone in the voice, so that they can get accustomed to seeing you approaching. Next give their noses a good rub, so that they may learn to recognize a man by his smell. Shortly after this it is a good idea to stroke the skin all over, and sprinkle them with neat wine to make them more companionable to their ploughman; it is good too to put your hand on the belly and under the thighs, to prevent their being alarmed if they are touched in this way later on; also to get rid of ticks, which habitually fasten on the thighs. While doing this, the trainer should stand at the side, so as to keep out of reach of the hoof. After this, open the jaws, pull out the tongue and rub the whole mouth and palate thoroughly with salt, and put down the animals' throats a pound-size lump of meal moistened with well-salted dripping, and pour into their jaws a pint of wine apiece by means of a horn; with this type of coaxing treatment they take three days to become tame, and on the fourth day, allow you to put a yoke on them. The yoke is pierced by the branch of a tree instead of a yoke-beam; from time to time a weight is also attached to it, so that the animal's capacity for endurance may be tested by the greater effort required. After experiments of this kind, the oxen should be yoked to an empty wagon and gradually made to do longer journeys with loads. Thus thoroughly broken in, they should later on be started on the plough, but on land already tilled, so that they may not be frightened at the outset by the difficulty of the task, and to avoid bruising their still tender necks by the hard breaking of the fallow. I gave instructions in my first book for the method to be used by the ploughman in training the ox for ploughing. Care must be taken to prevent the ox striking anyone with hoof or horn during his training; unless precautions are taken against this, it will never be possible to eradicate faults of this kind, even though the animal has been broken in.

The regime prescribed here is to be followed if no trained oxen are on hand; in that event the method of breaking in which I follow on my own farm is more streamlined, and more reliable. When we are getting a young bullock accustomed to the wagon or the plough, we take and yoke with the untrained animal the strongest and most docile of our trained oxen, which holds it back if it presses forward, and pulls it forward if it lags behind. Indeed, if we can take the trouble to construct a yoke to which three animals can be attached, by means of this contraption we shall achieve the result of forcing even recalcitrant oxen to take on the heaviest tasks. For when a lazy bullock is yoked between two veterans and is forced to till the ground once the plough has been attached, he has no chance of disobeying orders. If he gets in a temper and leaps forward, he is checked by the will of the other two; or, if he halts while the others are walking on, he follows even against his will; or again, if he tries to lie down, he is lifted up and dragged on by his more powerful companions. As a result, under compulsion from all sides he gives up his obstinacy, and only a few blows are needed to induce him to put up with hard toil.

VI(h) On pig-rearing

Varro, *On Farming* II.4.13–20

The fertility of a sow for breeding is usually estimated from her first litter, as she does not vary very much in later ones. As to the rearing of piglings, which is called *porculatio*, they are allowed to stay with their mother for two months. After that, when they are capable of feeding themselves, they are separated from her. Pigs born in winter grow thin, because of the cold, and because the mothers, having but little milk and, in consequence, finding their teats bruised by their teeth, push them away.

Every sow should have a sty to herself, and rear only her own litter, because she does not drive away the pigs of a strange litter; if therefore they get mixed up she deteriorates in breeding. Her year is naturally divided into two parts, since she farrows twice a year, being pregnant for four months, and suckling for two.

The sty should be constructed about three feet high, and a little more than that in width; and no lower than this above the ground in case a sow when pregnant tries to jump out, and so miscarries. The height should be such as to enable the swineherd to take in the whole sty at a glance, and prevent any pigling from being crushed by his mother, and to clean out the sty easily. The sty should have a door, with a threshold one-and-a-third feet high to prevent the piglings jumping over it whenever the mother goes out. It is the swineherd's job, every time he cleans out the sty, to throw in sand or some similar absorbent material to soak up the moisture. When a sow has farrowed, he must keep up her strength with more generous rations, to make it easier for her to maintain her milk supply. They are usually fed about 2 lb of barley apiece, soaked in water; some double this amount, giving it morning and evening if they have nothing else to give them . . . Weaners are usually given grape-skins and grape-stalks if the farm supplies them . . .

At breeding-time, care is taken to see that the sows drink twice a day for the sake of the milk. They say that a sow should bear as many pigs as she has teats; if she bears less, she will be less profitable; if more, something is portended. The most ancient portent of this kind on record is the sow of Aeneas at Lavinium, which bore thirty white pigs; and thirty years later the people of Lavinium founded the town of Alba . . . A sow can feed eight little pigs at first, but when they have gained weight, experienced breeders commonly remove half of them, as the mother cannot supply enough milk, nor can the litter get enough food to gain strength. For the first ten days after delivery the sow is not taken out of the sty, except to drink. After this time they are allowed to go out to pasture in some spot close to the farmstead, so that they can return frequently to suckle their brood. When the latter have grown big, they are allowed to follow their mother when she goes out to feed, but when they come home, they are separated from their mother, and fed apart, so that they may learn to do without the nursing mother, which they manage in ten days. The swineherd should train them to do everything in obedience to the sound of the horn. After first shutting them in, they open the doors whenever the horn is sounded, so that they can come out to a place where barley meal has been poured out in a line. In this way less is wasted than if it is piled in a heap, and more pigs can get at it more easily. The object, we are informed, of having them come together at the sound of the horn is to prevent them getting lost when dispersed in wooded country.

VI(j) Transhumance in Euboea

Dio Chrysostom, *Discourses* VII.10–15

As we walked along he told me of his affairs and of the life he led with his wife and children. 'You see, there are two of us, stranger,' he said, 'living in the same place. Each of us is married to a sister of the other, and we have sons and daughters by them. We get most of our livelihood from hunting, and work only a small plot. You see the place isn't ours, either by inheritance, or acquired by our own efforts. Our fathers, though free men, were just as poor as we are—

hired herdsmen, looking after the cattle belonging to a wealthy landowner, an islander from hereabouts, a man who owned many droves of horses and cattle, many flocks of sheep, and many excellent fields as well, plus many other possessions, and all these hills to boot. Now when he died and his property was confiscated—they say he was executed by the emperor because of his great wealth—they immediately drove off his stock for slaughter, including, in addition to his herd, our own few head of cattle, and nobody has paid us our wages. So we just had to stay on at the place where we had been keeping our cattle, and had erected some huts and a stockaded enclosure for the calves; not very big or strongly made—just what would do for the summer, I suppose; in winter, you see, we pastured our cattle in the lowlands, where we had sufficient grazing, and a good deal of hay put by; but in the summer we used to drive them into the mountains. This was their favourite place for making their steadings; the plain sloped inwards from both sides to form a deep, shady glen, in the middle of which flowed a quiet stream in which the cows and their calves could wade easily. There was an abundant supply of pure water bubbling up from a spring near by; and in summertime, a breeze always blew steadily through the glen. The neighbouring glades were soft and moist, breeding hardly a gadfly or other cattle pest. Many beautiful meadows stretched beneath tall, well spaced out trees, and the entire area abounded in lush vegetation all summer long, so that the cattle did not range very far afield. For these reasons they made a regular habit of keeping their herd there.

VI(k) Sheep on the public highway

Fronto, *Letters* II.12

Marcus Caesar to his teacher . . .
. . . But what was the story I was going to tell you? When father was on the way home from the vineyards I jumped on my horse as I always do and set off down the road. I hadn't gone far when I saw a large flock of sheep huddled together in the road as they do in places where the way is narrow. There were four dogs and two shepherds and nothing else. Then one of the shepherds, when he spotted our little gang riding up, shouted to the other one, 'See them horsemen? They're the biggest robbers out!' When I heard this I dug my spurs into my horse and galloped straight into the sheep. They scattered in panic all over the show baa-ing and bleating. One of the shepherds hurled his crook and it struck the man riding behind me. We beat it! The shepherd who was worried about losing his sheep broke his crook!

D'you think I'm inventing this? It's true—and there's a lot more I could tell you, but the boy has just come to say my bath is ready. Goodbye, beloved teacher. You are a very fine and remarkable person. I think of you with the greatest affection.

VII

THE CHANGING PATTERNS
OF RURAL LIFE

The harsh realities of life on the land for those who sweated over their daily labours with plough, mattock or sickle are seldom treated to more than a cursory glance by writers preoccupied with the physical comforts and diversions of those who reaped the financial rewards of those labours (see Introduction, p. 8 ff.). The material selected in this chapter deals with some of the more important aspects of agrarian history in Greece and Italy, and the topics include the land reform programmes of Solon at Athens and Tiberius Gracchus at Rome.

The pressure of population on the available food supply meant that adverse weather conditions produced local food shortages among subsistence farmers, while major natural disasters such as drought and pestilence resulted in widespread famines, aggravated by inadequate means of communication. Hence the emphasis on these topics (Ch. VII n, o) along with that of rural depopulation (Ch. VII f, g, m). By contrast we have an extract from Varro's lengthy account (*On Farming*, Book III) of luxury farming (Ch. VII j), and Martial's description of the highly productive estate of his friend Faustinus in that home of luxurious living, the seaside resort of Baiae (Ch. VII h).

VII(a) Land reform in sixth century Athens

Solon, *Elegies* xxxvii in Aristotle, *Constitution of Athens* xii.4

O Mighty Mother of the Olympian Gods,
Dark Earth, thou best can witness, from whose breast
I swept the pillars broadcast planted there,
And made them free, who had been slaves of yore.
And many a man whom fraud or law had sold
Far from his god-built land, an outcast slave,
I brought back home to Athens; yes and some,
Exiles from home through debt's oppressive load,
Speaking no more the dear Athenian tongue,

But wandering far and wide, I brought again;
And those that here in vilest servitude
Trembling before their masters' whims I set them free,
Thus yoking might and right in harmony,
Since by the force of law I won my ends
And kept my promise . . . Equal laws I gave
To evil men and good, with even hand
Drawing straight Justice for the lot of each.
But had another held the goad as I,
One in whose heart were guile and greed,
He'd not have kept the people back from strife.

F. G. KENYON

VII(b) Solon's land reform

Plutarch, *Life of Solon* XIII.2–3; XV.2–5

All the common people were in debt to the wealthy. They either worked their lands for them, paying them one sixth of the increase (that is why they were called *Hektemors* or Sixth partners and *Thetes* or labourers), or else they took loans on the security of their persons, and could be seized by their creditors; some became slaves in their own country, and others were sold abroad. Many, too, were forced to sell their own children (there was no law to prevent this), or go into exile, because of the brutality of the moneylenders. But the majority —and they were the sturdiest—began to form a faction, urging one another not to put up with their plight, but to choose as their leader someone they could trust, liberate the defaulters, divide up the land afresh, and make a radical change in the form of the government . . .

Now later writers say that the Athenians used to cover up the ugly face of things by the use of decent and uplifting language giving them polite and attractive names. Thus they called whores 'companions', taxes 'contributions', the garrison of a city its 'guard', and the prison a 'chamber'. But Solon was the first, it would appear, to employ this device, when he called his cancellation of debts a 'shaking off of burdens'. The first item in his political programme was an enactment that existing debts should be wiped out, and that in future nobody should lend money on the security of the person . . . In his poems he makes the proud boast that he 'dug up the record-stones planted everywhere; before, the earth was in bondage; now she is free'. And concerning the citizens who had been seized for debt, some he restored from foreign exile 'no longer uttering their native Attic speech, so long and far they had been wandering, and some who were at home were suffering shameful misery'.

VII(c) The tax-free farm

Aristotle, *Constitution of Athens* XVI

It was while Peisistratos was travelling on this business that the affair of the man on Mount Hymettus who was farming the piece of land afterwards known as Tax-Free Farm, occurred. He saw a man digging and working at a piece of land which was nothing but rocks. Surprised by what he saw he ordered his servant to ask the man what profit he got out of the farm. 'All the aches and pains in existence', was the reply, 'and of these aches and pains Peisistratos must get his tithe.' The man gave his reply without knowing who the questioner was, but Peisistratos was delighted by his outspokenness and his industry, and relieved him of all taxes.

VII(d) The land reform bill of Tiberius Gracchus: Plutarch's version

Plutarch, *Tiberius Gracchus* VIII–IX

Whenever the Romans annexed territory from their neighbours after a war, they usually put part of it up for auction; the remainder was made common land, and was distributed among the poorest and most destitute of their citizens, who were allowed to cultivate it on payment of a nominal rent to the Treasury. When the well-to-do began to outbid and force out the poor by offering higher rents, a law was passed which made it illegal for anyone to hold more than 310 acres of land. This measure for a time restrained the avarice of the rich, and protected the poor, who were enabled to remain on the land they had rented, so that each of them could keep the holdings originally allotted to him.

But after a time the rich men in each district, by using fictitious names, contrived to make over many of these holdings to themselves, until in the end they openly took possession of the greater part of the land under their own names. The poor, finding themselves forced off the land, became more and more unwilling to volunteer for service in the army, or even to raise children. The result was a rapid diminution in the class of free subsistence farmers throughout Italy, their place being taken by gangs of foreign slaves, employed by the rich to cultivate the holdings from which they had forced out the free citizens.

VII(e) The background to land reform in Italy: Appian's version

Appian, *Civil Wars* I.I.7

The Romans as they subjugated Italy, region by region, used to take possession of a part of the territory and establish towns there, or enrol colonists from among their own people to occupy already existing towns. Their intention was to use these places as outposts; as for the land acquired by fighting, they at once assigned the cultivated part of it to the settlers, or sold it, or rented it out. With regard, however, to the part which then lay devastated by war—and this generally the greater part of it—they were not yet at leisure to allocate it; so they made proclamation that in the meantime anyone willing to work it might do so against a charge on the annual crops, consisting of ten per cent of the sown, and twenty per cent of the planted crops. On those who kept animals a charge was levied for both large and small cattle. Their aim in this was to replenish the Italian stock, which they regarded as having great endurance, so that they might have allies of their own kin. In the event, however, the situation swung round and had a reverse effect upon them; for the rich, getting possession of the greater part of the unallocated territories, and encouraged by the lapse of time to believe that they would never be dispossessed, and getting possession of adjoining strips, together with the allotments of their poor neighbours, partly by purchase and persuasion, partly by forcible means, came to farm vast tracts instead of single units, using slaves as farm-workers and herdsmen so as to prevent free citizens being drawn off the land into the armed forces. At the same time the acquisition of slaves was a very lucrative business by reason of their offspring, who increased because they were exempt from military service. Thus some powerful individuals became extremely wealthy, and the slave population increased throughout the country, while the Italian people dwindled both in numbers and in strength, under the crushing burdens of poverty, taxes and military service. If they got any respite from their afflictions, they passed their time in idleness, because the land was in the possession of the rich, who used slaves instead of free men to cultivate it.

VII(f) Depopulation in Latium

Livy VI.12

The dictator, though he perceived that he had a more serious contest on his hands at home than abroad, held a levy of troops and set off for the Pomptine territory, the area to which he understood the Volscian army had orders to proceed. His motive in this was neither the need for a rapid advance nor the belief that a victory and a triumph would add strength to his dictatorship. I have no doubt that the unbroken series of campaigns against the Volscians will not only provoke in my readers a sense of surfeit, but will also cause them to share with me that feeling of astonishment which came upon me as I reviewed the authorities who stand closer to these events, that after these innumerable defeats the Volscians and Aequians had enough combatants left. The point has been passed over without comment by the ancient writers, but how could I possibly go beyond passing an opinion which anyone is entitled to make and vouch for the truth of this matter? There are various possible explanations: either during intervals of peace they made use of successive generations of men of military age to initiate hostilities; or their levies of troops were not always drawn from the same tribal groups, although wars were set on foot by the same nation, or there existed incredible numbers of free citizens in those areas which now are only redeemed from total depopulation by slaves.

VII(g) Depopulation of Italy

Lucan, *Pharsalia* 1.24–32

Now Rome, if so great a lust for impious war possesses you, now that you have put the entire globe under the laws of Latium, turn your hands against yourself. You have not yet come to lack enemies. But now that the walls of her cities are with their houses half demolished, and great stones lie on their tumbled battlements, and there is no one left to protect their homes, and their scattered inhabitants wander in her ancient towns, now that Italy lies bristling with thickets, her soil for many years all untilled, and there are no hands to cultivate the earth that calls out for their help, the responsibility for these terrible calamities will not be yours, Pyrrhus, nor that of Carthage. It has been the fate of no foreigners to plumb the depths of armed conflict. The wounds of civil strife are deeply rooted.

VII(h) Devastation in Italy

Lucan, *Pharsalia* VII.387–411

These hands shall wreak havoc such as no generation can wipe out, nor any race of men repair, though all their years were free from the sword. This conflict will overthrow peoples that are yet to be, and, by depriving them of birth, will sweep away the nations of the generation now coming into the world. Then the whole Latin Name will be a legend. Their ruins, mantled with dust, will scarce be able to point to the site of Gabii, Veii or Cora, or the household shrines of

Alba or the sacred hearth of Laurentum. The countryside will be empty, and there no senator will lodge, save under compulsion of the dark, and complaining that it was Numa's bidding. It is not age that has eaten away these monuments of past deeds, and left them to crumble. In all these uninhabited cities we can see the guilt of civil war. To what small numbers is the crowd of mankind reduced? We who are born in every part of the earth can populate neither our cities nor our fields. The crops of Italy are tilled by convict labourers; in our ancestral abodes, houses stand crumbling, destined to kill no one when they fall; Rome is not peopled by men of her own stock, but filled to the brim with the world's dregs, and we have brought her so low that civil war cannot be fought, in spite of all her population. Pharsalia is the author of this great mischief. Let the deadly names of Cannae and Allia, accursed for so long in the calendar of Rome, give way to this. Rome has marked down the dates of less bearable disasters. This date she has resolved to blot out of her mind.

VII(j) On luxury estates

Varro, *On Farming* III.2.5–18

'Are you really telling us that this villa of yours on the edge of the Campus Martius is merely useful, and isn't more lavishly equipped with luxuries than all the villas owned by everyone in Reate all put together? Why, your villa is plastered with pictures, and with statues too, while mine hasn't a trace of Lysippus or Antiphilus, but plenty of the hoer and the shepherd. Furthermore, my villa has a large farm attached, and one which has been kept clean by cultivation, while yours hasn't a field or an ox or a mare. To sum up, what has your country house got that resembles the one your grandfather and greatgrandfather owned? It has never seen, as that one did, hay in the hay-loft, a vintage in the cellar, or a corn-harvest in the bins. The fact that a building is outside the city does not make it a country house any more than it does the houses of those who live outside the Porta Flumentana or in the Aemiliana.'

To this Appian replied with a smile: 'As I don't know what a country house is, please enlighten me, so that I shall not come a cropper through lack of foresight: I want to buy one near Ostia from Marcus Seius. If buildings are not villas unless they contain that £4,000 as you showed me at your place, I shall be buying a week-end cottage on the seashore instead of a villa. My friend here, Lucius Merula, set me on to acquire this house when he said, after spending several days at Seius' place, that he'd never been entertained in a villa that he liked more, although he'd seen no pictures, not a single statue of bronze or marble, nor yet any apparatus for pressing grapes, nor oil-jars nor oil-mills.' 'Why then,' asked Axius, looking at Merula, 'what sort of villa is that which has neither the furnishings of a town house nor the equipment of a farmhouse?' 'Well', said Merula, 'isn't your house on the bend of the river Velinus, which has never been seen by a painter or a plasterer, to be regarded as no less a villa than the one in the Rosea which is decorated with plaster work in the best taste, and of which you are the joint owner with your ass?' Axius indicated with a nod that a house which was merely a farmhouse was just as much a villa as one which was both a farmhouse and a city residence; he also wanted to know what inference his friend drew from these facts. 'What inference?' said he; 'why, if your farm in the Rosea is to receive approval because animals are pastured there, and if it is correctly called a 'villa', because cattle are fed and stalled in it, the estate I'm talking about should also with equal reason be called a 'villa', because large profits are obtained by feeding animals there. What does it matter whether you get your profit from sheep or birds? . . . There are two kinds of feeding; the one, which includes cattle-raising, is carried on in the fields, the other around the steading; the latter includes the rearing of hens, doves, bees and the other animals usually fed there. On this topic Mago of Carthage and Cassius Dionysius and other writers have both written special treatises and made scattered references in their books; and these Seius has apparently read to such good purpose that he gets more profit out of a single villa than other people get out of a whole estate. 'You are quite right', said Merula; 'I've seen there large flocks of geese, chickens, pigeons, cranes and peafowl, as well as masses of dormice, fish, wild boars and other game. His bookkeeper—a freedman: he once waited on Varro and used to entertain me when his master was away— told me that they used to give him a profit of more than 50,000 sesterces a year.' When Axius showed surprise I remarked to him: 'You surely know my maternal aunt's estate in the Sabine country, at the twenty-fourth milestone from Rome on the Via Salaria?' 'I certainly do,' he replied, 'since I usually break my journey there in the summer around noon, while on my way from Reate to Rome, and I usually pitch my camp there in winter at night, when I'm on my way from there to the city.' 'Well,' I said, 'from the aviary alone in this villa 5,000 fieldfares were sold at 3 denarii apiece; that section brought in that year 60,000 sesterces, which is twice as much as your farm of 200 iugera at Reate brings in.' 'What? Sixty?' exclaimed Axius, 'Sixty? Sixty! You're joking!' 'Sixty,' I repeated. 'But to make such a killing as that,' he said, 'you'll need a public banquet, or somebody's triumph, like that of Metellus Scipio at that time, or the club dinners that are now so innumerable that they send up the price of provisions to dizzy heights.' 'If you don't look for this return,' I said, 'in all succeeding years, your aviary will not, I hope, go bankrupt on you; and does it happen, with current trends, that you often incur a loss? How few are the years in which you don't see a banquet or a triumph, or in which the clubs don't feast?' 'To be sure,' he said, 'current high life creates what you might call a daily banquet inside the gates of Rome. Was it not Lucius Abuccius, who is, as you know, a very cultured man, whose satires are cast in the Lucilian mould, who used to say that his farm in the Albano district was always beaten by his villa in the animals it bred, for the land returned less than HS 10,000 and the villa more than 20,000. It was he too who stated that if he could have got hold of a villa in a place of his own choosing, at the seaside, he would have made more than *HS* 100,000 out of it. Come now, didn't Marcus Cato, when he took the guardianship of Lucullus recently, sell fish out of the latter's fishponds to the tune of 40,000?' 'My dear Merula', said Axius, 'take me on, I beg you, as a pupil in the art of feeding animals inside the villa.' 'Certainly,' he replied, 'I'll start as soon as you promise to pay the fee.' 'Agreed,' he said, 'you may have it today, or later many times over out of this animal-feeding of yours.' 'I believe you'll pay,' replied Appius, 'the moment one of these animals dies, a goose, I expect or a peacock!' 'Well,' said Axius, 'what difference does it make if you do eat birds or fishes that have died, seeing that we never eat them unless they're dead? But please lead me on the road to the scientific practice of the art of farm feeding, and expound its scope and method.'

VII(k) A very productive estate

Martial, *Epigrams* III.58

Our friend Faustinus' country place at Baiae, Bassus, keeps unproductive no spacious fields laid out in useless myrtle hedges, and clumps of clipped box, but rejoices in a real bit of rough country. Here every corner is packed tight with corn, and many a pot is fragrant with old-fashioned autumn smells. Here, when November is over, and winter close upon us, the shaggy pruner brings home late gathered grapes. Fierce bulls bellow in the upland valley, and the calf with hornless brow itches for battle. The whole motley crowd of the untidy farmyard are milling around, the shrill goose, the spangled peacock, and the bird that owes its name to its flaming feathers, the painted partridge, the speckled guinea-fowl, and the impious Colchians' pheasant. Proud roosters tread their Rhodian dames. The cotes re-echo with the noise of pigeons, on this side moans the ring-dove, on that the glossy turtle-dove. Greedily the porkers follow the bailiff's wife, and the tender lamb waits for its dam's distended udder. Homeborn infant slaves encircle the clear-burning hearth, and abundant piles of timber gleam before the household gods on festal days. The lazy innkeeper does not sicken with pallid ease, nor does the oily wrestling-master waste the oil, but he stretches a crafty net for greedy fieldfares, or with quivering line takes and draws out the fish, or brings home the doe entangled in his toils. The easily worked garden keeps the town slaves cheerfully busy and, without orders from the overseer, even the wanton long-curled pages gladly obey the manager; even the effeminate eunuch enjoys his task. Nor does the country visitor come empty-handed; this one brings pale honey in its comb, and a pyramid of cheese from Sassina's forest; that one offers sleep-filled dormice; another the bleating offspring of a shaggy dam; another capons forced to abandon love. The strapping daughters of honest farmers offer in a wicker basket their mothers' gifts. When work is over a cheerful neighbour is invited to dine;

no niggardly table keeps the feasting for tomorrow; all dine, and the well-fed steward need not envy the well-wined guest. But you in the suburbs are the owner of elegant starvation, and all you can see from your high tower are laurels. You are at ease; your Priapus fears no thief, and your vine-dresser you ration on corn bought in town, and lazily cart to your frescoed villa cabbages, eggs, fowls, fruits, cheese, and new wine. Should this place be called a farm, or a town house away from town?

VII(l) Farm tenancy problems
Pliny, *Letters* IX.37

I must remain here to organize the letting of my farms on long leases. I shall have to adopt a new system of leasing. During the past five years, in spite of my making considerable reductions in the rents, the arrears have increased; as a result most of my tenants have given up all concern for reducing their debts, because they have abandoned any hope of paying back what they owe; they even seize and consume the produce, convinced as they are that they will gain nothing by keeping it.

I must therefore face up to this increasing evil and find a cure. One method would be to let out the farms on a share-cropping basis instead of a money rent, and then make some of my servants overseers to keep a watch on the harvest. Certainly the fairest return to the investor is that offered by soil, climate and seasons. But this demands strict honesty, sharp eyes, and a large labour force. However, I must make the experiment and try out all possible varieties of remedy for a deep-seated malady.

VII(m) Neglect of land and depopulation in Greece
Dio Chrysostom, *Discourses* VII (*Euboicus*).33–5; 38–9

Then another man came forward, a decent fellow, to judge from what he said and from his appearance. He first asked the crowd to be silent, and they obeyed. Then in gentle tones he said that those who cultivated the country's unfarmed land, and put it in good order, were doing nothing wrong: on the contrary, they deserved praise. They should direct their anger, not against people who built on public land and planted trees on it, but against those who despoiled it. 'At this very moment, gentlemen,' he went on, 'almost two-thirds of our land is abandoned, through a combination of neglect and depopulation. I too have a large acreage, as I believe some others have, not only in the mountains, but in the plains as well, and if anyone were willing to cultivate it, I should not only give him the opportunity to do so gratis, but would gladly pay him money as well. It is obvious that my holdings have increased in value; at the same time the sight of land in occupation and under the plough is a pleasing one, while unworked land is not only a useless asset to its owner, but suggests that he has suffered some misfortune... At the moment even the land just outside the city gate is completely wild, and a disgraceful sight, like land set in the middle of a wilderness, not in the suburbs of a city, while most of the ground inside the walls is either plough or pasture. You can surely see for yourselves that they [viz. the orators] have converted your gymnasium into a ploughed field, so that the Herakles and many other statues, some of which are those of heroes, others of gods, are hidden by the corn. You see also day after day the sheep belonging to this orator breaking into the market place at dawn and grazing around the Council Chamber, and the executive buildings. That is why, when strangers first come to our city, they either laugh at her or pity her.'

VII(n) The Maktar reaper

Corpus of Latin Inscriptions VIII.11824 (=*ILS*, 7457, 3 ff.)

I was born in a poor household; my father was poor, with neither property nor a house of his own. From the day of my birth I have lived by working my land; neither my land nor I has ever had a rest. When the season came round for the harvest to be ripe, I was the first to cut the stalks. When the gangs of harvesters appeared in the fields, making for the Numidians of Cirta, or the fields of Jupiter, I was still the first to harvest my field, ahead of all the rest, leaving thick sheaves at my back. I cut the corn for others under the raging sun ahead of all the rest, leaving thick sheaves behind my back. Twelve years' harvests I cut under the raging sun, and through my services I was afterwards made foreman, and for eleven years I commanded teams of harvesters, and our company cut the fields of Numidia. Hard work, and contentment with little, finally brought me a home with a farmstead, and my home lacks nothing in wealth. Furthermore, my career has achieved the rewards of office; I too have been enrolled among the senators of the city, and chosen by them I took my seat in the temple of that body, and from a poor farm boy I actually became a censor. I have seen my children and my grandchildren grow up around me, and I have enjoyed years distinguished by the merits of my career—years have brought no accusation from any malicious tongue. Learn, mortals, how to live free from accusations. Thus has he deserved to die who has lived honourably.

VII(o) A severe famine in Italy

Symmachus, *Reports*

The law of our fathers had honoured the Vestal Virgins and the servants of the gods by granting them the wherewithal to enjoy a modest livelihood and reasonable privileges. This gift remained intact right up to the time of those worthless dealers in small change, who have diverted the rewards of sacred chastity to pay the wages of common porters. This was followed by a wretched harvest. It was not the lands that were at fault; no blame should be attached to the winds. Rust did not spoil the crops, nor did weed choke the standing corn. It was blasphemy that dried up the year's crops ... People were kept alive by eating the twigs of forest trees; the country folk were starving and rushed to the oak trees [viz. for acorns].

VII(p) A famine relieved

Ambrose, *Duties of the Clergy* III.45–7

But they, too, who would forbid the city to strangers cannot have our approval. They would expel them at the very time when they ought to help, and separate them from the trade of their common parent. They would refuse them a share in the produce meant for all, and avert the intercourse that has already begun; and they are unwilling, in a time of necessity, to give those with whom they have enjoyed their rights in common, a share in what they themselves have. Beasts do not drive out beasts, yet man shuts out man. Wild beasts and animals consider food which the earth supplies to be common to all. They all give assistance to those like themselves; and man, who ought to think nothing human foreign to himself, fights against his own. How much better did he act who, having already reached an advanced age, when the city was suffering from famine, and, as is common in such cases, the people demanded that strangers should be forbidden the city, having the office of the prefectship of the city which is higher than the rest, called together the officials and richer men, and demanded that they should take counsel for the public welfare. He said that it was as cruel a thing for the strangers to be expelled as for one man to be cast off by another, and to be refused food when dying. We do not allow our dogs to come to our table and leave them unfed, yet we shut out a man. How unprofitable, again, it is for the world that so many people perish, whom some deadly plague carries off! How unprofitable for their city that so large a number should perish, who were wont to be helpful either in paying contributions or in carrying on business. Another's hunger is profitable to no man, nor to put off the day of help as long as possible and to do nothing to check the want. Nay more, when so many of the cultivators of the soil are gone, when so many labourers are dying, the corn supplies will fail for the future. Shall we then expel those who are wont to supply us with food? Are we unwilling to feed in a time of need those who have fed us all along? How great is the assistance which they supply even at this time! 'Not by bread alone does man live.' They are even our own family; many of them even are our own kindred. Let us make some return for what we have received. But perhaps we fear that want may increase. First of all, I answer, mercy never fails, but always finds means of help. Next, let us make up for the corn supplies which are to be granted to them, by a subscription. Let us put that right with our gold. And, again, must we not buy other cultivators of the soil if we lose these? How much cheaper is it to feed than to buy a working-man! Where, too, can one obtain, where find a man to take the place of the former? And suppose one finds him, do not forget that, with an ignorant man used to different ways, one may fill up the place in point of numbers, but not as regards the work to be done.

VIII

RURAL CULTS AND FESTIVALS

The first three passages (Ch. VIII a–c) have been chosen to convey something of the general flavour of a festival occasion, including its most important element, the procession in honour of the patron deity. These are followed by detailed accounts of well-known country festivals, including the cleansing of the fields, which has something in common with the old English Beating of the Bounds (Ch. VIII d and e), the Boundary Festival (The *Terminalia*) (Ch. VIII f), and the Feast of Anna Perenna (Ch. VIII g); this part concludes with prayers to the gods of the countryside (Ch. VIII j and k), and Horace's fine Ode to the Well of Bandusia (Ch. VIII l).

VIII(a) A country feast

Aristophanes, *The Acharnians* 241–79

DIKAIOPOLIS: Keep holy silence, all. Let the basket-bearer go forward just a little. Let Xanthias hold the phallus-pole erect.

MOTHER: Set down your basket, daughter, and let us begin the rite.

DAUGHTER: Hand me the ladle, mother, so that I may pour the sauce over the cake.

DIK: 'Tis well! Lord Dionysos, grant me, now set free from all campaigning, to marshal this procession, and offer sacrifice with my household, and keep the rural feast of Dionysos auspiciously. And may this thirty-year truce turn out well for me.

MOTHER: Come, daughter, mind you carry the basket sweetly, my sweet, with savory-eating look. Happy the man who weds you, and gets you with kittens that can fart as well as you at daybreak. Go forward, and take care they don't snatch your jewels in the crowd.

DIK: Xanthias, your job is to fall into line behind the basket-bearer, holding the phallus upright, the pair of you. I'll follow and sing the phallic hymn. You, wife, look on from the rooftop. Forward! O Phales, companion of the orgies of Bacchus, night-wanderer, adulterer, pederast, for the past five years I've not been able to call upon you. But now with a will I return to my home, now that I've made a private peace for myself, and said goodbye to cares and fights and Lamachuses. Sweeter by far it is Phales, my Phales, to surprise Thratta, the pretty wood-carrier, Strymodorus' slave girl, stealing wood from Mount Phelleus, to catch her by the waist, lift her up and throw her down and take the kernel out of her. O Phales, my Phales, if you will drink with us and get blotto, you will drink at daybreak a goblet in honour of Peace; and my shield will be hung up in the chimney.

VIII(b) Procession of the Eleusinian initiates

Aristophanes, *The Frogs* 312–51

XANTHIAS: Hey, you!

DIONYSOS: What's up?

XAN: Don't you hear it?

DION: What?

XAN: The sound of flutes.

DION: Yes, I do, and a highly mystical whiff of torches wafted over in my direction; but let's take cover quietly and listen.

CHORUS OF INITIATES: Iacchos, oh! Iacchos, oh! Iacchos!

XAN: That's the very thing, master; these are the initiates he told us about, at their games right here! Why, they're singing the Iacchos song, the one they sing in the agora.

DION: Yes, I think they are. Better keep still though, until we know for certain.

CHO: Iacchos, who dost dwell here in venerated resting places, Iacchos, oh! Iacchos! Come to this meadow to direct your devout fellow revellers in the dance, shaking on your head a burgeoning wreath laden with myrtle berries, and with bold foot beating time to the playful measure, sharing in abundance the Muses' charm, a dance pure and holy to pious initiates.

XAN: O Lady, much revered daughter of Demeter, what a delicious whiff of pork came over to me! Please keep still there, in case you even get a smell of tripe.

CHO: Kindle the torches to flame, for in our hands there is carried, O Iacchos, oh, Iacchos!—the light-bringing star of our nightly revel. The meadow is on fire with fire! Old men's knees are bounding! Thanks to this holy service they are shaking off the burden of care and the weight of the endless round of years. Advance with blazing torch, and lead forth the youthful chorus to the flowery, marshy plain.

VIII(c) On the way to a festival

Theocritus, *Idylls* VII.1–51

One time when Eukritos and I were going from town to Haleis, and Amyntas joined us to make a third, Phrasidamos and Antigenes, the two sons of Lykopeus were making harvest offerings; they were the finest of those ennobled by their descent from Klytia and Chalkon, who planted his knee firmly against the rock and made the spring of Burina well up beneath his foot; and alongside the spring, poplars and elms with green foliage arches in profusion above, wove the fabric of a shady grove.

We had not yet got as much as half way along our road, nor had the tomb of Brasilas come in sight when, by the Muses' favour, we fell in with a traveller, a man of Kydonia, and a man of quality. His name was Lycidas, and he was a goatherd, and no one that saw him could have mistaken his identity; he looked every inch a goatherd. On his shoulders he wore the tawny pelt of a thick-haired shaggy goat, smelling of fresh rennet, and across his chest was thrown an ancient tunic with a broad belt; in his right hand he gripped a crooked club of wild olive. With a quiet grin and a twinkle in his eye, he spoke to us, and laughter played round his lips. 'Where on earth are you footing it to in the middle of the day, Simichides, when even the lizard sleeps in the wall, and the tomb-crested larks stay at home? Are you pressing on uninvited to some banquet, or hurrying off to some townsman's wine-press, for as you go every pebble springs away singing from your shoes.' I answered him: 'Friend Lycidas, everyone says that you are by far the best of pipers among the herdsmen and harvesters; and this makes me glad. Yet when I think of it I reckon I'm as good a piper as you are. We are on our way to a harvest festival; friends of mine are holding a feast for fair-robed Demeter, presenting the first-fruits of their plenty. For the goddess has piled up their threshing-floor with barley in full, rich measure. But come; the way and the day are here for you and us to share. Let us sing our country songs, and each perhaps will do the other a good turn, I too am the clear voice of the Muses; and everyone calls me the finest of singers; but I am not so quick to believe what I am told, no by Da! According to my way of thinking, I am not yet the equal in song of the excellent Sikelidas from Samos, nor of Philetas, but compete with them like a frog among crickets.' That's what I said, and with a purpose. With a pleasant laugh the goatherd replied, 'I'll make you a present of this cudgel, for you are a sprig of Zeus, fashioned for truth. I detest the builder who tries to raise his house as high as Mount Kromadon, and I hate those cocks of the Muses who waste their efforts crowing against the Bard of Chios. But come, let us at once begin our country singing, Simichides, and I—see friend whether it pleases you, the song I worked out lately on the mountainside . . .'

VIII(d) Purification of the fields

Cato, *On Farming* C X L I

The purification of the fields must be done in the following way: Order the piglambcalf (*suovetaurilia*) to be led around, and say, 'That with the help of the gods success may crown our labours, I bid you, Manius, to take care to purify my farm, my fields, my land, with the piglambcalf, whenever you think it best for them to be either led or carried round. 'First offer a prayer, with wine, to Janus and Jupiter, and then say 'Father Mars, I pray and beseech you that you will be propitious and merciful to me, my house, and our household; that is why I have ordered a piglambcalf to be led round my fields, my land, my farm; that you may keep away, fend off and remove sickness, both visible and invisible, barrenness and ruin, blight and unseasonable weather; and that you may allow my harvest, my corn, my vineyard and plantations to flourish and yield abundantly; protect my shepherds and my flocks, and grant good health and strength to me, my house, and my household. For this purpose, in order to purify my farm, my land, my folds ... be honoured to accept the offering of these suckling victims.

VIII(e) The cleansing of the fields

Tibullus, *Elegies* II.I.I–24

Keep silence, all: we purify the fruits and fields
according to the usage of our ancestors.
Come, Bacchus, with the sweet grapes hanging from your horns,
and bind your brow with wheaten garland, Ceres.
Let rest the land in holy daylight, let the ploughman rest,
hard labour over, while the share hangs idle.
Unstrap the yokes. Today the oxen are to stand
At laden mangers, garlanded with flowers.
Serve God in every action. Let no woman dare
To lay hand on the daily weight of wool.
I charge all you whom Venus granted joy last night
To stand apart and not approach the altar.
The Gods love purity. Come wearing clean clothes
and take in clean hands water from the spring.

See, the sacred lamb advances to the shining altar,
leading the white procession wreathed with olive.
Gods of our fathers, we purge the fields and the field-workers.

Drive away all evil from our boundaries.
Let no cornland cheat the harvest with deceptive weeds,
No swift wolf terrify the laggard lamb.
Then the cheerful farmer, trusting his full fields,
will pile the fire with large logs, while a troop
of servants' children, token of their master's plenty,
Play before it, building houses of sticks.

GUY LEE

VIII(f) Festival of the Terminalia
Ovid, *Calendar* 11.638–60

When the night has passed let the god who divides the arable lands with his marker receive the honour usually bestowed on him. Terminus, whether you are a stone, or a post buried in the field, you have been worshipped (*numen habes*) from of old. You are crowned by the two owners on opposite sides, who bring you two garlands and two cakes. An altar is erected. Hither the farmer's country wife brings with her own hands on a sherd the fire which she has taken from her own warm hearth. The old man chops up wood, and skilfully piles up the faggots, and tries to plant the branches in the solid ground. Then he gets the kindling flames going with dry bark; his boy stands by holding the broad basket. After he has tossed corn three times into the fire his little daughter offers the pieces of honeycomb. Others hold out jars of wine; portions of each are cast into the flames. The company, dressed in white, look on in holy silence. At the meeting of the boundaries Terminus is sprinkled with the blood of a slaughtered lamb, and makes no complaint when a sucking-pig is given to him. The honest neighbours meet and hold festival, and sing your praises, holy Terminus. You set bounds to nations and cities and kingdoms; without you every field will be a subject of wrangling.

VIII(g) Festival of Anna Perenna
Ovid, *Calendar* 111.523–42

On the Ides [of March] is held the happy feast of Anna Perenna, not far from your banks, O Tiber, river from a foreign land. The common folk arrive; and scattered all around amid the green grass they drink, every Jack beside his Jill. Some rough it under the open sky; a few pitch tents. Some have made leafy cabins out of branches; others have set up reeds in place of stout pillars, and spreading out their togas have laid them on the top. But they grow warm with sun and wine, and they pray for as many years as the cups they take, and they count up how many they have drunk. There you will find a man who drains as many goblets as Nestor counted years, and a woman who would turn into a Sibyl if it could be done by cups. There they also sing the airs they learnt in the theatres, beating time to their words with fast-moving hands. They set down the mixing-bowl, and lead the clumsy dances, while the smart sweetheart skips about with hair unbound. On the way home they totter, a sight for ordinary folk, and the crowd that meets them calls them 'happy'. I ran into the procession the other day: I thought this story worth telling; a drunken old woman was hauling along a drunken old man!

VIII(h) The gods have transformed country life

Tibullus, *Elegies* ii.1.37–66.

Country I sing and country Gods. Life as their disciple
Ceased to drive away hunger with the acorn.
They taught men first to tie rafters together
and roof a little home with green thatch.
They were the first to teach the bull his bondage
and place the wheel beneath the wagon's weight.
Then wild fare was forgotten; fruit-trees then were planted
and kitchen-gardens drank the channelled stream;
Then the trampled grapes gave golden liquor;
Then sober water mixed with carefree wine.
The country brings us harvest in the shimmering heat
When Earth each year lays down her yellow hair.
In springtime, in the country, light bees are busy bearing
Flowers to the hive to fill the combs with honey.
It was a farmer, wearied with continual ploughing,
Who first sang country words in fixed metre
and after feasting measured on the first oaten pipe
A tune to play to gods he had adorned.
A farmer too, O Bacchus, daubed with cinnabar,
Improvised your dithyramb, receiving
That memorable trophy from a full fold, the flock's leader,
A he goat to augment his modest means.
It was a country child who first fashioned of spring flowers
A diadem to crown the ancient Lares.
And in the country too, future trouble for tender girls,
soft fleeces line the backs of milk-white sheep.
Hence woman's work, hence woollen stint and distaff,
The spindle-twisting yarn beneath the thumb,

The weaver's song, Minerva's constant votary,
and the loom's clatter as the weights collide.

GUY LEE

VIII(j) Prayers to the country gods
Ovid, *Calendar* IV.742–82

Say: 'Take thought both for these cattle and their master; let all harm be driven
away and fly from my stables. If I have fed my sheep on holy ground, or sat
down beneath a sacred tree, or if with my knowledge my sheep have browsed
on graves; if I have entered a forbidden grove, or if the nymphs and the half-
goat god have been put to flight on seeing me; if my billhook has robbed a
sacred copse of a shade-giving branch to fill a basket with leaves for a sick sheep,
grant pardon for my misdoing. Lay it not to my charge if I have sheltered my
flock in a rustic shrine till the hail gave over, and may I not suffer for having
shattered the quiet of the pools.

Forgive me, nymphs, if galloping hooves have sullied your waters. Goddess,
propitiate on our behalf the springs and their guardian spirits; propitiate the
gods dispersed through every grove. May we not see the Dryads, nor Diana's
bath, nor Faunus, when he lies in the fields at noonday. Drive diseases far away.
May men and beasts be healthy, and healthy too the sagacious pack of watch
dogs. May I drive home my flock as numerous as they were at daybreak, and
may I not complain as I bring back fleeces snatched away from the wolf. Let
dire hunger not come my way. Let there be abundance of grain, and leaves,
and of water both for washing and for drinking. Full udders let me milk; may
my cheese bring me money; may the wicker-work sieve let through the liquid
whey. May the ram be randy, and his mate conceive and bear, and many a lamb
inhabit my fold. And let the yield of wool not chafe the skins of lasses, nor
roughen the tenderest of hands. May my prayer be fulfilled, and year by year
we shall make big cakes for Pales, the Mistress of Shepherds.'

These are the prayers with which to appease the goddess; say these words
four times over, facing the East, and wash your hands in fresh dew. Then you
may set a wooden bowl, to serve as a mixing-bowl, and bring the snow-white
milk and the purple must. Later you must with swift foot carry your eager
limbs across the burning heaps of crackling straw.

VIII(k) A prayer to Faunus

Horace, *Odes* III.18

O Faun-god, wooer of each nymph that flees,
Across my land, across those sunny leas,
Tread thou benign, and all my flock's increase
    Bless ere thou go—
If each full year a tender kid be slain,
If Venus' mate, the bowl, be charged amain
With wine, and incense thick the altar stain
    Of long ago.
The herds disport upon the grassy ground,
When in thy name December's Nones come round;
Idling on meads the thorp, with steers unbound,
    Its joy doth show.
Amid emboldened lambs the wolf roams free,
The forest sheds its leafage wild for thee,
And thrice the delver stamps his foot in glee
    On earth, his foe.

J. WIGHT DUFF
(*A Literary History of Rome to the
Close of the Golden Age*, London, 1967)

VIII(l) Bandusia's well

Horace, *Odes* III.13

Bandusia's Well, that crystal dost outshine
Worthy art thou of festal wine and wreath!
An offered kid tomorrow shall be thine,
Whose swelling brows his earliest horns unsheath,
And mark him for the feats of love and strife;
In vain; for this same youngling from the fold
Of playful goats shall with his crimson life
Incarnadine thy waters fresh and cold,
The blazing Dog-star's unrelenting hour
Can touch thee not; to roaming herd or bulls
O'er-plied by plough, thou giv'st a shady bower
Thou shalt be one of Earth's renowned pools;

For I shall sing thy grotto ilex-crowned,
Whence fall thy waters of the babbling sound.

J. WIGHT DUFF
(*A Literary History of Rome to the
Close of the Golden Age*, London, 1967)

IX

PRIVATE PLEASURES IN THE COUNTRYSIDE

In this chapter we turn our attention from the public to the private aspects of country living, beginning with the joyous scene from Aristophanes' *Peace*, in which the vinedresser Trygaeus gives thanks to the gods for the gift of peace as he prepares to return rejoicing to his farm after ten long years of enforced exile, and ending with two pieces from the *Letters* of Sidonius, on holidaying in the grand style of the fifth century, almost a thousand years later! The selection includes Theocritus' masterly Tenth Idyll, which contains no artificial 'pastoral' flavour, but is filled with the sweat and exhaustion of the harvest. Apart from the lovely Lityerses Song, this poem could take its place in Chapter V.

The passages from the four Augustan poets (Ch. IX e–j) cover a wide spectrum of response to rural themes. The countryside in which Tibullus envisages his mistress presiding over the labours of the farm (Ch. IX e) is no Arcadia, but the poet's own: Tibullus owned the small estate at Pedum to the east of Rome on which he was born—'a fact which makes him one of the few truly Latin poets, as opposed to Italians like Horace and Ovid, or provincials like Catullus and Virgil' (Guy Lee, Tibullus: *Elegies*, 1975). Tibullus shares with that other genuine countryman, Virgil, a belief in the simple country gods and their traditional rites (Ch. IX h) where the references to the ancient cults of trees, of the Lares, of Ceres the corn-goddess and Priapus the garden-god, are no literary conceits, but the manifestation of a genuine piety. Virgil's description (Ch. IX f) of the flourishing garden made out of derelict land contains a characteristic moral: the old man who created this oasis, and serves as a model for all gardeners by being first with everything he grew, had come as a settler from Cilicia in Asia, and so was almost certainly a pirate' (Wilkinson, *The Georgics of Virgil*, London, 1969). Horace's story of the frugal yeoman farmer dispossessed of his land, who practises, as well as preaches, the Stoic doctrine of meeting with a stout heart the buffetings of outrageous fortune, is, characteristically, added as a vigorous illustration of the views expounded in the Satire.

With Martial the reader is transported into a different atmosphere, resembling that of Georgian England. Each of the two pieces chosen (Ch. IX k and l) has its own pungent flavour, and each is a gem of unforced elegance.

References to the pleasures of the seaside are uncommon; our single passage on the theme (Ch. IX n) is a lucky accident: the dialogue in which it occurs is the only work by its author to have survived, and recounts the story of the conversion to Christianity of his friend Caecilius, which occurred during a walk along the beach near Ostia. Minucius' account of how they ran across a group of youngsters playing at skimstones shows that he had a genuine talent for descriptive narrative, and a keen eye (one might have said a novelist's eye) for significant detail, whether he is caught up in the swirling movement of advancing and retreating waves, or in the game the boys are playing.

IX(a) Peace returns to the farm

Aristophanes, *Peace* 556–600

TRYGAEUS: Listen, good folk! Let the farmers take their tools and be off to the fields with all speed, but without sword, spear or javelin; for everything here is brimming with the mellow joys of peace. Come, let everyone raise Apollo's victory-song, and go to work in the fields.

CHORUS: O longed-for Day, the desire of all just men and husbandmen. I have gazed on you with joy; and now I want to greet my vines, and the fig-trees I planted in my youth I long to embrace after so long an absence.

TRYG: Well now comrades, our first task is to adore the goddess who has taken away from us the crests and gorgons; then let us buy a nice little piece of salt fish to eat in the field, and hasten to our farms.

CHO: By Poseidon! What a fine crowd they make, and dense as the crust of a cake, and nimble as guests on their way to a feast.

TRYG: See how their mattocks are there all ready to hand, and how their pitchforks glisten in the sunlight. How well they set the rows of vines in order! I too have long been aching to get into the country and break up my little plot with the hoe. Friends, you recall the happy life of former times that Peace once granted us, remember those figs fresh and dried, the myrtles, the sweet grapes, the violets near the spring, and the olives for which we pined. Worship, adore the goddess now for her bounties.

CHO: Hail! hail! beloved goddess, we are overjoyed at your return. Longing for you subdued me utterly, heavenly one, as I longed to creep back into my fields once more. . . . You were our greatest blessing, O Peace so much desired by all who spend our lives in tilling the earth; you are our sole support. In former days when you reigned over us, we enjoyed a thousand fair delights without expense; you were the farmer's wheaten groats, and his salvation. That is why our vineyards, our young fig plantations, and everything we've planted will hail you with delight and greet your coming.

IX(b) The harvesters

Theocritus, *Idylls* x

MILON: Husbandman Boukaios, what's the matter with you, poor lad? You can't keep your swathe straight, as you used to, and you don't keep up with your neighbour in the reaping, but get left behind, like a ewe when a thorn has pricked her foot. What are you going to be like in the evening or even in the afternoon if right now at the start you don't get your teeth into your row?

BOUKAIOS: Milo, you that reap late in the day, chip of the unyielding rock, did you never feel a longing for an absent sweetheart?

MI: Never! What's a working man got to do with a longing for something that has nothing to do with his job?

BOU: Didn't love ever keep you lying awake?

MI: No, and I hope it never will; it's a bad business for a dog to get a liking for hide.

BOU: But I've been in love for more than ten days already, Milo.

MI: You can drink your fill straight from the cask, that's clear; but I get the dregs, and not enough of that.

BOU: That's why the ground in front of my door is all unhoed since the sowing.

MI: And which of the lasses is it that tortures you so?

BOU: Polipitas' girl, the one that was piping to the reapers on Hippokion's farm the other day.

MI: God reveals the sinner! You've got what you've been wanting all this time. So that praying mantis of a wench will be cuddling you all night long.

BOU: You're starting to poke fun at me. But the god of wealth isn't the only god who's blind. There's the scatterbrain love god as well. Stop talking big!

MI: I'm not talking big. Just put your crop on the ground, and strike up a love-song for the lass. You'll work more contentedly so; indeed you were a singer in the old days.

BOU (*sings*): Pierian Muses, hymn with me the slender lass; everything you touch, goddesses, you refine. Charming Bombyka, everyone calls you gipsy, lean and sunburnt, while I alone call you honey-coloured. The violet is dark, and so is the lettered hyacinth, yet in garlands they are said to be tops! The goat chases the snail-clover, the wolf the goat, the crane the plough, and I'm crazy for you! If only I were as rich as Croesus in the fairy tale, we'd both be standing in gold as gifts to Aphrodite— you with your pipes, and a rosebud or an apple, and I with new clothes and shoes on my feet, Charming Bombyka, your feet are like knuckle-bones, your voice is like honey, and words fail me to describe your ways!

MIL: Boukaios was a maker of lovely songs, and has kept us in the dark! How well he measured out the pattern of his tune! Alas, my poor beard, I grew it all in vain. Mark too the lines of golden Lityerses.

THE LITYERSES SONG

Demeter, rich in fruit and grain, grant that the crop may be easy to reap and a bumper one. Binders, bind up your sheaves, in case someone passes by and says: 'These are good-for-nothing chaps; here's another wage-waster.' See that the cut end of your swathe faces the north wind or the west. This way the ear grows fat. When you thresh the grain, avoid the midday siesta; that's the time when the ear parts easiest from the stalk. But when you reap, set to when the lark awakens, and stop when he goes to bed, but take a rest in the heat. Enviable is the frog's life, lads. He doesn't trouble about anyone filling his goblet; he has liquor beside him galore. Boil the lentils better, stingy steward, in case you chop your fingers splitting cummin-seed.

That's the stuff for men who work in the sun to sing. As for your starveling love-affair, Boukaios, tell your mother about it when she stirs in bed at dawning.

IX(c) Scipio Africanus' bath house at Liternum

Seneca, *Letters* LXXXVI

I have inspected the house which is constructed of hewn stone, the wall which encloses a forest; the towers as well, buttressed out on both sides for the purpose of defending the house; the cistern, concealed among buildings and shrubbery, large enough to keep a whole army supplied, and the tiny little bath house, buried in gloom, according to the old style: our ancestors didn't believe in taking a hot bath except in the dark. So I felt a keen sense of pleasure as I contrasted Scipio's habits with ours. Just think! In this tiny recess the 'Terror of Carthage', to whom Rome owes a vote of thanks for not being captured more than once, used to bathe a body exhausted by labour in the fields. He was in the habit of keeping himself on the go, and cultivating the soil with his own hands, as the good old Romans were wont to do. Beneath this dingy roof he stood; and this floor, mean as it is, supported his weight . . .

In this bath of Scipio's there are tiny chinks—you cannot call them windows —cut out of the stone wall in such a way as to let in light without weakening the fortifications; nowadays, however, people regard baths as fit only for moths unless they have been designed to trap the sunshine all day long through the widest of windows, if men cannot simultaneously bathe and get a tan, and if they cannot look out from their bath-tubs over expanses of land and sea. So it goes; the establishments which drew crowds and won admiration when they were first opened are avoided and put back into the category of venerable antiques as soon as luxury has worked out some new device, to her own destruction. In the early days, however, there were few baths, and they were not fitted out with any ostentation ... How some folk nowadays condemn Scipio as a boor for not letting the daylight into his perspiring room through wide windows, nor roasting in the strong sunshine nor dawdling around until he could stew in the hot water! 'Poor sod,' they declare, 'he didn't know how to live! He never bathed in filtered water; it was often turbid, and after rain almost muddy!' But it didn't matter much to Scipio if he had to bathe that way; he went there to wash off sweat, not ointment. And how do you reckon certain people will answer me? They will say: 'I don't envy Scipio; that was truly an exile's life—to put up with baths like those!' Friend, if you were wiser, you would know that Scipio didn't bathe every day. It is stated by those who have made reports to us on the old-time manners of Rome that the Romans washed only their arms and legs every day—because these were the parts of the body that gathered dirt in their daily work—and bathed all over only once a week. At this point someone will retort: 'Yes, pretty dirty fellows they certainly were! How they must have stunk! But they smelled of the camp, the farm, and of heroism. Now that spick-and-span bathing establishments have been devised, men are really dirtier than they were before. What says Horatius Flaccus, when he wants to describe a scoundrel, one who is notorious for his extreme indulgence? He says: 'Buccillus smells of perfume.' Show me a Buccillus in these days; his smell would be the veritable goat-smell—he would take the place of the Gargonius with whom Horace in the same passage contrasted him. It is nowadays not enough to use ointment, unless you put on a fresh coat two or three times a day, to keep it from evaporating on the body. But why should a man boast of this perfume as if it were his own?

IX(d) The Elder Cato on country pleasures
Cicero, On Old Age XVI.56-8

I could dwell at length on all the many delights of country pursuits, but I realize that I have already said more than enough. You must forgive me! My enthusiasm for farming has carried me away. Besides, old age is naturally rather garrulous—I say this in order to avoid acquitting it of every fault! Well then, this was the sort of life that Manius Curius led in his remaining years, after his triumphs over the Samnites, the Sabines and Pyrrhus. As I fix my gaze on his country house—it is not far from my own—I cannot adequately admire the self-control of the man, and the moral standards of the age in which he lived ... Have we then any reason to feel sorry for these men of the olden days in their old age, men who took delight in cultivating the soil? For my part at least I am inclined to think that the farmer's life is the happiest of all, not merely from the point of view of the job he does, which benefits the whole of mankind, but also because of the pleasure I mentioned earlier, and the abundance it provides of everything connected with the nurture of human beings, and even with the worship of the gods; and since there are people who take delight in these activities, I have said this, so that I may now make my peace with pleasure. The really good, hard-working proprietor always has his storeroom and cellars filled with oil, wine and provisions. His entire farm prospers, abounding in pork, goat's meat, lamb, poultry, milk, cheese and honey. There is also the kitchen garden, which the farmers themselves call 'the second flitch'. Hawking and hunting too, in leisure periods, provide the seasoning for their dainties.

IX(e) The poet dreams of farming with his mistress

Tibullus, *Elegies* 1.5.21–36

I who wearing woollen fillet and unbelted tunic
In the silent night made nine vows to Diana,
I paid them all, and now someone else enjoys my love
And profits from my prayers, the lucky man.
In my folly I had dreamed that the lucky life was mine
If you recovered, but the God willed otherwise.
'I'll farm,' I thought, 'and Delia will be there to guard the grain
While the sun-baked floor threshes harvest in the heat.
Or she will watch the grapes for me in the laden troughs
and the white new wine pressed by trampling feet.
She will learn to count the sheep. The children of the house-slaves
Will learn to play and prattle on a loving mistress's lap.
She will offer to the farmer God grapes for the wines,
Ears for the standing corn, a victim for the flock.
She can rule us all, take charge of everything
And I'll enjoy non-entity at home.
When my Messalla comes to see us, Delia will pick him
Delicious apples from our choicest trees,
And in the great man's honour attend to all his needs,
Prepare a dinner for him and wait on him herself.'

GUY LEE

IX(f) An old man's well-kept plot
Virgil, *Georgics* IV.125–46

I mind how once, 'neath the shade of Oebalia's lofty towers, where dark Galaesus bathes the yellow fields, I saw an old man of Corycus, who had a few acres of abandoned land, the soil too poor for ploughing, useless for grazing and unfit for vines; yet he, while planting pot-herbs here and there amid the scrub, and round them white lilies, and verbena and scanty poppies, by his energy matched the wealth of kings, and ever, as he came home at night, he would pile his table high with unbought produce. He was the first to pick roses in spring, and apples in autumn, and when harsh winter was already cracking the rocks with cold, and curbing the flow of streams with ice, he was already cutting the blossom of the soft hyacinth, taunting summer for her lateness and the west winds for delaying.

And so he was the first to abound in full-grown bees and a powerful swarm, and first to squeeze the combs and gather the fermenting honey. Limes he had, and laurustinus in plenty, and as many as were the fruits with which in early blossoming the vigorous tree had clad herself, so many she retained full ripe in autumn. Also he planted out in rows late elm-shoots, and plums already fruiting and planes already giving shade to drinkers.

IX(g) Cynthia on the farm
Propertius, *Elegies* II.19

Although you're leaving Rome against my wishes, Cynthia,
　　I'm glad that while away you'll live in rural wilds.
There'll be no young seducer in unpolluted meadows
　　whose blandishments might press you to be false to me,
neither will any brawl start up outside your windows
　　nor will your sleep be soured by shouts of *Cynthia*.
You'll be alone, your gaze on solitary mountains
　　and cattle and a humble tenant-farmer's fields.
There you will have no shows or theatres to seduce you,
　　or temple-courts, most frequent cause of your misdeeds.
There you can gaze all day at teams of oxen ploughing
　　and vines shedding their hair to expert pruning-knives.
There too in some rude shrine you'll dedicate rare incense,
　　while at the rustic altar a kid is sacrificed,
and then you can take part with bare legs in the dances—
　　provided there's no risk from an intrusive male.

Myself, I'll turn to hunting. Already I look forward
    to being Diana's convert, renouncing Venus' vows.
Commencing wild beast catcher, I'll hang a pine with antlers
    and learn to give commands to an eager pack of hounds—
it being understood I'd *not* beard the huge lion
    or rashly come to close quarters with wild boars.
The limit of my daring would be to net the gentle
    hare and fix the bird with a reed fowling-rod,
where fair Clitumnus roofs his river with beloved
    trees and where his wave washes the snow-white kine.
Whenever you've a mind to try something, remember
    that after a few dawns I'll come to you, my life.
Here neither lonely woods nor errant rivers pouring
    down from moss-grown passes will ever put me off
from murmuring your name in ritual repetition
    lest anyone should wish an absent lover's harm.

GUY LEE

IX(h) The poet longs for a quiet life

Tibullus, *Elegies* I.1–14; 25–8; 33–6

Wealth let others gather for themselves in yellow gold
and acquire great acres of cultivated land—
scared on active service, in contact with the enemy,
their sleep put to flight by the blare of trumpet-calls.
But let my general poverty transfer *me* to inaction,
so long as fire glows always in my hearth.
Early in the season I should set the tender vines
and the tall maidens with a peasant's practised hand.
Hope would never fail me, but deliver an abundance
of produce, brimming over the vat at vintage time.
For I pray at every solitary tree-stump in the fields
or old stone at the cross-roads that is garlanded with flowers;
and the first of every fruit the new season raises for me
is offered at the feet of the farmer God. . .
If only, now at last, I can live content with little
and not be handed over to the never-ending road,
but avoid the summer rising of the Dog-star, in the shadow
of a tree, beside the waters of a running stream! . . .
But let the robber and the wolf spare my little flock
and plunder the big folds,

for here I never fail to purify my shepherd
and sprinkle kindly Pales every year with milk.
GUY LEE

IX(j) A contented countryman

Horace, *Satires* II.2.112–36

But, deeper to impress this useful truth,
I knew the sage Ofellus in my youth
Living, when wealthy, at no larger rate
Than in his present more contracted state.
I saw the hardy hireling till the ground
('Twas once his own estate); and while around
His cattle grazed, and children listening stood,
The cheerful swain his pleasing tale pursued.
    On working days I had no idle treat,
But a smok'd leg of pork and greens I eat;
Yet when arrived some long-expected guest,
Or rainy weather gave an hour of rest,
If a kind neighbour then a visit paid,
An entertainment more profuse I made;
Though with a kid, or pullet, well content,
Ne'er for luxurious fish to Rome I sent;
With nuts and figs I crowned the cheerful board,
The largest that the season could afford,
The social glass went round with cheerfulness,
And our sole rule was to avoid excess.
Our due libations were to Ceres paid,
To bless our corn, and fill the rising blade,
While the gay wine dispell'd each anxious care,
And smooth'd the wrinkled forehead too severe.
    Let fortune rage, and new disorders make,
From such a life how little can she take!
Or have we liv'd at a more frugal rate
Since this new stranger seized on our estate?
Nature will no perpetual heir assign,
Or make the farm his property or mine.
He turn'd us out; but follies all his own,
Or law-suits and their knaveries unknown,
Or, all his follies and his law-suits past,
Some long-lived heir shall turn him out at last.
The farm, once mine, now bears Umbrenus' name,

The use alone, not property, we claim;
Then be not with your present loss deprest,
And meet the future with undaunted breast.

PHILIP FRANCIS
(Horace, *Satires and Epistles*, trans.
Philip Francis, London, 1747)

IX(k) Views from an upland suburban farm

Martial, *Epigrams* iv.64

The Fields that Julius my namesake know
For owner, though they be not few, I trow,
On the Janiculum more happy rest
Than all the fabled islands of the Blest.
Their sheltered acres from the hills rise high
Whose level summit takes the clearer sky;
And even when thick with mists the valley drown,
It shines with brightness that is all its own.
While in the night the farmhouse gables seem
To lift to heaven to catch the starry gleam.
On this side you may see the Seven Hills,
And mark the space that one great city fills,
The heights of Tusculum and Alba's home,
And all the cool suburban haunts of Rome,
Red roofs, and old Fidenae, and the trees
Where, with a maiden's blood, we Anna please,
On that, the Flaminian and Salarian Way
Their noiseless stream of travellers display,
Whose distant wheels disturb not your repose,
And though close by the sacred Tiber flows
Beneath the Milvian Bridge, no bargemen's noise
Nor sailor's shout breaks in upon your joys.
Whether 'tis country or a town estate
Its master most doth grace it, and his gate
Is ever open, generous and free;
You'd think it might your own dominion be.

F. A. WRIGHT
(Martial, *Epigrams*, trans. J. A. Pott and
F. A. Wright, London and New York, 1924)

IX(l) A poet's invitation to dinner at his farm

Martial, *Epigrams* x.48

The priests proclaim the hour at Isis' shrine
When guard is changed, 'tis time to bath and dine.
Cool are the baths too hot an hour ago,
At the sixth hour with Nero's heat they glow.
Friends, are you ready? There are five of you,
My horse-shoe couch holds seven—bring Lupus too.
My bailiff's wife has gathered mallows light
And garden treasures for the feast tonight;
Sliced leeks there are, dwarf lettuce, cool and smooth,
Rocket to stimulate, and mint to soothe.
Anchovies crowned with egg, and dressed with rue,
And pickled pork with tunny-fish will do
To whet the appetite, and following these
A kid the ravening wolf had hoped to seize;
Rissoles that need no carving-knife are there,
Spring cabbages and beans—the labourer's fare.
A fowl, a ham that twice has served; and last,
Sweet apples come to crown the whole repast.
Then, as to home-grown wine I know 'tis clear,
Free from all crust, as it was made this year.
Gay jest and kindly wit shall thus beget,
With naught to bring repentance or regret.
Safely we'll gossip of the racing season,
The cup shall stir no guest of mine to treason.

F. A. WRIGHT
(Martial, *Epigrams*, trans. J. A. Pott and
F. A. Wright, London and New York, 1924)

IX(m) An old man's country retreat

Pliny, *Letters* III.1

I don't believe I've ever passed the time so pleasantly as I did on a recent visit
to Spurinna; indeed there isn't anyone else whose examples I would prefer to
follow in my old age, if I am granted the privilege of reaching that estate. No
regime is as well-ordered as his ... Every morning he stays in bed for an hour
after daybreak, then calls for his shoes, and exercises both mind and body with

a three-mile walk. If he has friends staying, there are very fine conversations on the go; if not, a book is read to him, and this is sometimes done even when friends are present, provided they don't object. Then he settles down, the reading is continued, or preferably the conversation; after which he gets into his carriage, accompanied by his wife (a model to her sex) or one of his friends, a privilege I enjoyed quite recently... After a seven-mile drive he will walk an extra mile, then sit down again, or retire to his room and his writing: he composes the most accomplished lyrics in both Greek and Latin; they are remarkable for their charm, polish, and humour, and their charm is enhanced by the integrity of the author.

When bath time is announced (at three o'clock in winter, in summer at two), he strips for a walk in the sunshine, if there's no wind; then he has a long and vigorous session of ball play, this being the sort of exercise he employs to keep old age at bay. After his bath he lies down for a short break before dining, and listens while something rather light and soothing is read. During this time his friends are free to follow his regime or not, as they choose.

IX(n) An excursion to the seaside

Minucius Felix, *Octavius* III.2–6

This conversation took us to the half-way mark of our walk from the town to the open beach. A gentle ripple, spreading over the edge of the sands, levelled them into a sort of promenade. The sea, even on a windless day, is in constant motion, and drove towards the beach not in white crests, but in curling ripples, whose wayward motions we found perfectly delightful, as we allowed it to wet the soles of our feet at the water's edge, as the advancing breaker at one moment lapped our feet, and the next fell back and withdrew sucking back into itself. So we continued our quiet, leisurely progress, skirting the fringe of the gently curving beach, and whiling away the journey with stories...

But when, engrossed in conversation, we had gone a certain distance, we turned round and retraced our steps; and when we got to a place where some boats were lying quietly, propped up on oaken planks away from ground rot, we saw some youngsters competing enthusiastically in a game of tossing pot-sherds into the sea. The game consists of picking up a flat sherd from the beach, one made smooth by the action of the waves; you then grip the flat side with your fingers, then, bending forward low to the ground, you send it spinning as far as you can over the waves, so that the missile either skims the surface and swims along, gliding with a gentle impetus, or else it shaves the wavetops, glancing and leaping as it is supported by its continual jumps. The boy whose sherd went furthest and made the most leaps was the winner.

IX(o) A two-centre holiday

Sidonius, *Letters* II.9

I have had the most exquisitely pleasurable time visiting two highly attractive properties owned by highly cultivated men, Ferreolus and Apollinaris. Their estates have a common boundary, and their residences are not far apart, being connected by a road long enough to tire a pedestrian, but hardly long enough for a ride. The hills that rise above the buildings are cultivated by the vine-dresser and the olive-grower; you would imagine them to be Aracynthus and Nysa, mountains immortalized by poetry. The one house looks out over flat, open ground, the other on woods; yet while they differ in their situations, they both give similar pleasure. But why should I enlarge any further on the situation of the two farms, when what remains is to reveal the programme for my entertainment.

First of all, the most keen-eyed scouts were despatched to keep a sharp lookout on my return route, and both household staffs occupied not only the lines of the various public highways, but also the rough tracks and bypaths used by shepherds, so as to make it impossible for me to slip through the traps which their kindness had devised. I admit I was trapped, but by no means against my will; and I was at once forced to take an oath not to give a single thought to the resumption of my journey until a week had passed.

IX(p) Holidaying in style

Sidonius, *Letters* II.2.13–14

When you have finished your meal, a drawing room will bid you welcome, one which is a genuine summer room because it is not in the least a sun-trap, for, as it has only a north aspect, it admits daylight but no sunshine. Before you reach it, however, there is a narrow anteroom, where somnolent flunkeys can doze rather than slumber. How lovely it is here to have sounding in your ears the midday chirp of crickets, the croaking of frogs as evening descends, the honking of swans and geese in the early hours of rest, the crowing of cocks in the small hours; the birds of prophecy, the crows, greeting with their thrice-repeated call the red torch of rising Dawn, the nightingale warbling among the bushes in the half-light, and the swallow twittering among the rafters! To this concert of sound you are at liberty to add the pastoral Muse with the seven-holed pipe, which our sleepless mountain shepherds keep on sounding in nightlong singing competitions, among the belled flocks that bleat as they feed on the pastures. Yet all these changing modulations of sounds and voices will only fondle and titillate your slumber, and make it deeper.

X

HUNTING AND FISHING

The immense popularity of hunting and fishing as sporting activities among the leisured aristocracy of Greece and Rome is amply demonstrated by the volume of surviving illustrations in various forms of art, as well as in literature. An inscription on a gaming-table rates hunting top of a list of the four pleasures that make life worth living (*CIL*, VIII, 17938), and Cicero (*On Old Age*, 16.56) speaks of game-hunting and bird-catching as enjoyable pastimes for the elderly. On the other side of the medal, hunting and especially fishing provided a means of subsistence for the less privileged long before they were taken up as sports; and the professional hunters and the slave beaters remained to play essential roles in the pastimes of their masters. On the value of these activities, ancient attitudes vary considerably; Xenophon (Ch. X b fin.), and Oppian (Ch. X c, init.), have no doubts, while Cato supports hunting as an essential feature in the education of the young; like farming, it makes better soldiers of them. Polybius, on the other hand, objects to hunting as a useless occupation for the nobility.

The surviving literature on both subjects is almost as extensive as that on farming, and selection has therefore been difficult. All the technical writers have been included except Ovid, whose fishing manual (*Halieutica*) contains, not unexpectedly, practically nothing about fishing! Xenophon's spirited description of a hare hunt (Ch. X a) needs no commentary, and the same is true of the passages from Oppian (Ch. X c), Aelian (Ch. X h), and Ausonius (Ch. X j). The piece from Dio Chrysostom (Ch. X e) is in fact the continuation of the passage translated in Chapter VI (j); it gives the impression of being rather more worked up than the former, but makes very absorbing reading. Some readers may be surprised to learn that the making of artificial lures is no modern invention (Ch. X h).

The fourth piece in the collection from Theocritus (Ch. X g), generally regarded as the work of a gifted imitator, is a poem of great merit, conveying the authentic atmosphere of a fisherman's cabin, and skilfully portraying the characters of its two occupants. As for the well-known passage from Pliny's *Letters* (Ch. X f), there is surely nothing very eccentric in his behaviour: he is a professional writer with time on his hands, and a writer can always find a mechanical literary task to do while keeping much of his attention on the progress of the hunt, so as to be in at the kill! The purist will dismiss Chapter X (k) as an irrelevant intrusion. I am prepared, however, to justify its inclusion on the ground that it does contain some references to angling, as well as providing a fine display of its author's satirical talent.

X(a) On hare-hunting

Xenophon, *On Hunting* VI.11–17

The huntsman should go off to the field wearing light clothing and shoes, carrying a cudgel; the net-keeper should follow him. They should approach the field in silence, so that, in case the hare is somewhere close by, he may not make off on hearing voices. Having tied each of the hounds individually to the trees so that they can be easily slipped, he must set up his purse-nets and snares in the manner described above. After this the netman should stand guard while the huntsman proceeds to the 'lead-up' stage of the hunting; after making his vow to Apollo and Artemis the Huntress to give them a share of the bag, he must slip one hound, his cleverest tracker, at sunrise in winter, before dawn in summer, and at some intervening point at other times of the year. As soon as the hound picks up the trail from the maze of trails, a trail that runs straight ahead, he slips a second one. If the trail continues, he should slip the rest one by one at short intervals, and follow them without pushing them, calling on them severally by their names, but not frequently, in case they get excited prematurely. They will surge forward, joyous and eager, disentangling the different lines, double or triple, racing forward, now alongside, now across the same tracks—tracks interlaced or circular or straight or crooked, close-packed or scattered, familiar or unknown, running past each other, tails wagging fast, ears drooping and eyes flashing. When they are close to the hare, they will let the huntsman know by setting their whole body a-quiver from muzzle to stern, as they rush like warriors to the attack, racing past one another in competition, coursing together persistently, quickly bunching and as quickly fanning out, and rushing on again. At last they reach the hare in his form and will rush at him. Up he will leap and away, leaving the hounds barking and baying at him as he makes off. Then let the huntsman shout: 'Youi, youi, forrard away, hounds! Oh, well done! Oh, clever, clever!' Wrapping his cloak round his arm, and seizing his cudgel, he must follow the hounds as they go after the hare, and not try to head him off; that is a useless exercise. As he makes off, the hare, though quickly out of sight, usually doubles back to the place where they found him. Let him call out to the netman, 'Hit him, boy, hit him!' and the netman must tell him whether he is caught or not.

If the hare is caught in the first run, he must call in the hounds and look for another. But if not, the hunter must run with the hounds and not let up, but stick it out manfully. If the dogs light on him again in the pursuit, he must cry out, 'Well done, well done, hounds! After him, hounds!' If they have got so far in front of him that he cannot catch up with them by following up, and is completely out of the running, or if they are hovering close at hand or sticking to the trail but out of sight, he must find out by shouting to any man he comes across, 'Hullo there! Have you spotted the hounds?' And as soon as he discovers where they are, if he finds them on the track again, he must stand by and encourage them, calling every hound by name, using every variation in tone that he can muster, high and low, soft and loud.

X(b) Hunting the wild boar

Xenophon, *On Hunting* x.4–10; 19–21

First, then, when the hunting party has reached the place where they suppose the game to be lurking, having slipped a single Spartan hound, they must take the others on leash, and go round the area with her. As soon as she has found his spoor, they are to follow her, as she leads the way, in single file, keeping precisely to the line of the tracks. The hunters will find lots of signs of the animal—hoofprints in soft ground, broken saplings in dense bush, and tusk-marks in wooded country. The trail followed by the hounds will usually lead to a dense covert, the normal place for the animal to lie up, being warm in winter and cool in summer. The moment she discovers the lair, the hound will give tongue, but the boar is not usually roused. In that case, take the hound and tie her up with the rest of the pack at a good distance from the lair, and get the nets set up in the most likely places, suspending them in the forked branches of trees. Make a deep, protruding pocket in the net, inserting sticks on the inside to prop it up either side, so that daylight can penetrate as far as possible into the pocket through the meshes, making the interior as bright as possible when the boar charges at it. The guide-rope at the bottom must be secured to a strong tree, not to a branch, since the branches snap off when the trunks are bare. Where the ground provides poor anchorage, shore up each net at the bottom with wood, so that the boar may make his rush into the net, and not slip away.

When the nets are in position, let the hunting party make their way to the hounds, and unleash the whole pack; then taking their javelins and spears, let them advance. Let one man—the most experienced hunter—encourage the hounds, while the rest follow in good order, leaving wide gaps to allow the boar adequate space to pass between them; if he wheels about, and falls upon a close-packed line, they risk being gored: for he will vent his stored-up fury on anyone he encounters. As soon as the hounds are close to the lair, they will attack. Roused by the commotion, he will toss any hound that goes for him head on. He will run, and charge into the nets. If he doesn't, then you must go after him. If the ground where he is caught in the net is sloping, he will quickly get up; if it is level, he will immediately stand still, looking to himself. This is the moment for the hounds to press their attack; the huntsmen must throw their javelins at him warily, and pelt him with stones, forming a circle at some distance to the rear, until he drives hard enough to pull the guide-ropes of the net tight. Then let the most experienced and most powerful man in the party approach him in front and thrust his spear into him . . .

Another way of taking them is as follows. Nets are set in the defiles connecting the wooded dells with oak copses, winding glens, rocky places, or where there are passes running down into open meadows, marshes or pools. The net-keeper, spear in hand, watches the nets. The huntsmen bring up the hounds, searching for the most likely places. When the boar is found, they chase him. If he falls into a net, the net-keeper must take his spear, approach the boar, and use it as I have explained. If he doesn't fall into the net, he must chase him. The boar is also taken, in hot weather, by being run down by the hounds; for in spite of his enormous strength, the animal tires after a few bouts of prolonged hard breathing. Many hounds lose their lives in this type of hunting, and the hunters themselves are at risk, whenever the pursuit forces them to come up with the boar, spear in hand, when he is tired, or standing in water, or on a steep slope, or if he refuses to emerge from dense bush; for then neither nets nor any other obstacle will prevent him rushing at anyone who comes near him. Nevertheless, under these circumstances, they must face him, and display the pluck that induced them to apply themselves to this sport.

X(c) Trapping the lion

Oppian, *On Hunting* 77–111

But first, I beg you, lay to heart the noble lion hunt, and the valiant spirit of the hunters. First of all, they go and mark a spot where, among the caves, a roaring, well-maned lion has his lair, a great terror to cattle and to the herdsmen too. Next they trace the vast pathway with its well-worn footprints, on which the lion makes his way to the river to drink a sweet draught. Right there they dig a round pit, wide and large in circuit, and in the middle of the pit they build a great pillar, sheer and tall. From it they hang aloft a suckling lamb taken from its mother newly-delivered. And outside the pit they wreathe a wall around, built of close-packed boulders, so that the lion may not notice the cunning chasm as he draws near. And the high-hung suckling lamb bleats, and the sound of it smites the lion's hungry heart, and he rushes in search of it, exulting in his heart, eagerly following up the direction of the cry, and turning his gaze this way and that with fiery eyes. And quickly he comes close to the snare, and wheels around, and a great hunger urges him on, and immediately obeying his belly he leaps over the wall, and the round chasm envelops him all unwittingly, as he reaches the abyss of the unlooked-for pit. He wheels round in all directions, rushing ever backwards and forwards like a swift racehorse round the turning-post, controlled by the hands of the charioteer and by the bridle. And from their far-seen look-out post the hunters catch sight of him, and rush up, and with well-cut straps they let down a well-compacted woven cage, in which they put a piece of roast meat. And the lion, thinking to escape from the pit on the instant, leaps in, exultant, but for him is no return prepared. This is the way of hunting in the thirsty, alluvial land of Libya.

X(d) A humane view of hare-hunting

Arrian, *On Hunting* XVI.1–7

The best hares are those that have their forms in conspicuous and open situations; their audacity, it seems to me, prompts them to avoid concealment, and rather to challenge the hounds. When they are pursued, these same hares do not make for the glens or the woodland, even when these features are close at hand, enabling them to make an easy escape from danger, but press on into the open plains, competing with the hounds. And if slow hounds are following them, they run as long as they are being chased, but if fast ones, as long as their strength holds out. Often after they have turned aside into the plains, if they notice that a first-class hound is pursuing them so hard as to cast a shadow on them, they shake it off by doubling back on their tracks, or perhaps, if they happen to know a way down, they turn once again to the glens. There must be demonstrable proof that the hound has beaten the hare. I must tell you that the aim of your true sportsman with hounds is not to take the hare, but to engage her in a racing contest or combat, and they are satisfied if the hare encounters a hunter who will preserve her life. When some see her run for cover into a small clump of thistles, and others see her cowering and trembling with exhaustion, they call off the hounds, particularly if they have made a good contest of it. I myself, when following the chase on horseback, and coming up at the moment when the hare has been taken, have many a time let her go alive, have taken the hound away, tied it up and let the hare go free; if I arrived too late to save her, I have struck my forehead in grief for the slaying of a gallant opponent by the dogs. And this is the one point where I disagree with my namesake. I agree with him that to be present at the find and the run in a hunt would wipe out a thought of one's most cherished desire: but to see the hare overtaken is neither exciting nor pleasurable; it is obviously distressing, and certainly not an experience that exceeds the strongest desire of one's heart. But we must forgive dear old Xenophon for regarding the capture of the hare as a fine spectacle, since the fast Celtic hounds of our day were not known to him.

X(e) The seamy side of hunting
Dio Chrysostom, *Discourses* VII (*Euboicus*).15–20

Now at that time our fathers remained in their huts, until they could get themselves hired, or find some other work, and they lived on the produce of a very
small piece of land, which they chanced to have under cultivation, near the
cattle-yard. This was quite sufficient for them, as it was well stocked with
manure. Abandoning the cattle-farming, they took to hunting, sometimes on
their own, and sometimes using dogs; for two of the dogs that had followed the
cattle, after travelling a long way without a sight of the herdsman, had left the
herd and returned to the steading. At first they just followed, as if bent on
something other than the chase; and although when they saw wolves they would
give chase for a short distance, they would have nothing to do with boars or
deer. But whenever they sighted a bear, whether early or late in the day, they
would mass for an attack, barking and fending him off as if they were fighting a
man. And so, from tasting the blood of boars and deer, and often tasting their
flesh, they altered their habits late in life and learned to enjoy meat instead of
barley bread, stuffing themselves with it whenever any game was caught, and
otherwise going hungry, until finally they gave more attention to hunting,
pursuing with equal enthusiasm any animal they sighted, began to pick up the
scents and the trails somehow or other, and thus changed from sheepdogs into
a type of late-trained, rather slow hunting dogs! Then when winter came along,
there was no work in sight for the men whether they came down into the town
or into some village or other. So after reinforcing their huts, and tightening up
the fencing of the yard, they made a go of it this way, and worked the whole
of their plot, and the winter hunting turned out easier. The tracks were naturally
more visible, because they were printed in damp ground, and the snow made
them conspicuous from a distance, so that there was no need to take trouble
over the tracking, since there was a road leading to them, as you might say,
and the game was sluggish and more inclined to stay put. In addition to this,
hares and gazelles can be caught in their lairs.

X(f) Hunting and reading combined
Pliny, *Letters* 1.6

You will laugh, and well you may, when I tell you that your old pal has taken
three boars, and very fine ones at that. Have you really? you ask. I genuinely
have, and without giving up any of my lazy ways or my peace and quiet. I
was sitting beside the hunting nets: but alongside me I had, instead of hunting

spears, a stylus and writing tablets, working something out, and making notes, so that even if I come home empty-handed, I should at least return with note-books filled. There is no reason to look down on this kind of mental activity; indeed it's remarkable how one's wits are sharpened by bodily movement and exercise. The fact that one is alone surrounded by forest in the silence needed for hunting is a positive encouragement to thinking. So when you go hunting yourself, take your cue from me and bring your notebooks along with your lunch basket and your bottle; you'll find that Minerva haunts the mountains just as much as Diana does!

X(g) A dream of a fish
Theocritus, *Idyll* x x i

It is Poverty alone, Diophantus, that awakened the arts. She is the very instruc-tor of toil, for weighty cares do not allow working men to sleep; and if for some tiny fraction of the night a worker closes his eyes, anxieties assail him on the instant, and disturb his repose.

Two old fishermen had spread out for themselves a couch of dried kelp in their wattled hut, and were lying there together, propped up against the leafy wall. Near by them lay the instruments of their craft, the creels, rods, hooks, lines bedrabbled with seaweed, the weels, the lobster-pots of woven rushes, the seines, two oars, and an old fishing-smack on props. Beneath their heads was a thin matting, their clothes, their caps. No key they had, nor guard dog, for Poverty was their sentinel; there was no neighbour close by; and right beside their cabin the sea hemmed them in and the tide enclosed them . . .

(The fishermen wake up, and one of the pair, Asphalion, tells his companion about the dream he had the night before.)

'I went off to sleep before dark after our labours on the sea—I had not over-eaten, by the way, for we dined at the proper time, and did not overtax our stomachs. And I saw myself settled on a rock; and there I sat waiting for a fish, letting the treacherous bait dangle from my rod. A fish—one of the fat ones—reached up at it—dogs in their sleep dream of their quarry, and I dreamed of fish. He was hooked, and the blood flowed, and the rod was bent in my hand with his struggles. I leaned over with my arms outstretched, and had a mighty struggle—how was I to lift that monster of a fish with my weak tackle? Then, just to remind him of his wound, I pricked him gently, let go slack, and as he didn't run, I tightened. Well, I did win the encounter, and landed a golden fish, I tell you, plated all over with gold. I was gripped with terror, in case he might be some protégé of Poseidon, or perhaps some treasure of sea-green Amphitrite; and I gently released him off the hook, in case the barbs might remove the gold from his mouth . . . and vowed I'd never set foot in the sea again, but stay ashore and lord it over my gold. That woke me up. And now my friend, rivet your attention on the outcome of the story, for I'm terrified at the oath I swore!'

'Nay, never fear! You swore no oath, just as you never took the fish you saw. Your vision was a complete hallucination! But if, when you're awake, you seek out these monsters, there is hope of something from your dreams. Hunt flesh-and-blood fish, lest you die of starvation and your golden dreams!'

X(h) On fly-fishing

Aelian, *On the Nature of Animals* xv.1

There is a type of fishing in Macedonia, of which I have heard and know about. Between Beroea and Thessalonica flows a river, the Astraeus, containing speckled fish; as for their local name, you had better enquire from the Macedonians. They feed on flies which hover around the river—strange flies, quite different from any found elsewhere—not resembling wasps in appearance, nor can one identify them in shape with the insects called *anthedons* or wild bees, nor with hive bees; but they have some features in common with all of these. They are as bold as an ordinary fly; they are comparable in size with wild bees; their colour is taken from the wasp, and they buzz like bees. The local people habitually call them 'horsetails'. These flies settle on the river in search of their special food, but cannot avoid being seen by the fish swimming beneath. When therefore a fish notices a fly floating on the surface, he swims towards it very quietly under water, taking care not to disturb the surface, which would scare off his quarry. So he comes up on the side away from the sun, opens his mouth, gobbles up the fly like a wolf seizing a lamb out of the sheepfold, or an eagle taking a goose from the farmyard, and then slips back under the surface. Anglers are aware of this performance, but never use the natural fly as a bait; when the flies are handled, they lose their natural colour, their wings are battered and the fish will not feed on them. Anglers therefore make no use of the flies . . . but get the better of the fish by a skilful and cunning technique. They wrap some dark red wool round a hook, and attach to it two of the feathers that grow under the wattles of a cock, which are waxlike in colour. The rod and the line are both six feet long. When the decoy fly is lowered, the fish is attracted by the colour and rises frenziedly to catch the pretty object that will afford him a rare treat, but as he opens his jaws he is pierced by the hook, and gets small enjoyment of the feast when he is taken.

X(j) Angling on the Moselle

Ausonius, *The Moselle* 240-75

Now, when the bank offers easy approaches, a throng of predators scours all the deep places for fish, ill-protected—alas—by the river's sanctuary. This man, far out in midstream, trails his dripping nets and sweeps up the shoals, ensnared by their knotted folds; this man, when the river glides with peaceful flow, draws his seine-nets floating with the aid of cork markers; while over yonder on the rocks another leans over the water that flows underneath, and lets down the curved end of his pliant rod, casting hooks baited with deadly food. The wandering tribe of swimming fishes, knowing nothing of the trap, rushes upon them open-mouthed, and then, too late, their opened throats feel deep within the wounds made by the hidden steel. As they struggle, they are betrayed by the nodding of the rod as it responds to the tremulous vibrations of the quivering line. At once the boy neatly snatches his prey from the water with a hissing stroke, and plucks it slantwise; a whistling follows the strike, just like the wind that hisses and whistles when sometimes the air is shattered by a whip being whirled through empty air. The dripping catch flounders on the dry rocks, and cowers in fear before the deadly shafts of light-bringing day. While beneath his native water his strength stayed unimpaired, but weakened by our atmosphere he destroys his life as he pants out the air. Weakened now, his enfeebled body flaps quivering, and now his sluggish tail suffers its final throbs; his opened mouth closes no more; his panting gills give back the indrawn air, and expel the death-dealing breath of day. Even so, when the blast fans the flames of a smithy, the woollen valve which plays in the beechen hollows alternately draws in and stops the flow of air, now by one hole, now by the other. I myself have seen fish already quivering in their death-throes gather up their breath, and then, leaping high in the air, plunge somersaulting into the river beneath, gaining once more the waters they had despaired of reaching. Impatient at his loss, the boy dives recklessly from on high, and tries to recapture his prey as he swims senselessly.

X(k) An odd kind of angling

Lucian, *Fisherman* XLVII

PHILOSOPHY: What is the fellow planning to do? Baiting his hook with a fig and the gold, and sitting on the top of the wall, he's made a cast into the city! Have you decided to fish up the stones out of the Pelasgic shrine?

CANDOUR: Shut up, Philosophy, and wait till you see the catch! Poseidon, god of fishermen, and Amphitrite, send us up loads of fish! Ah! I spy a fine big pike—or maybe it's a gilt-head. Anyhow, he's coming up with his mouth wide open. He's scented the gold; now he's on to it, he's grabbed it; he's hooked! Up with him! You give a hand, too, Examiner, take hold of the line with me.

EXAMINER: He's up! Come, let me see what you are, my excellent fish. A dogfish, a cynic! Great Heavens, what teeth! So, my noble friend, you were caught hunting for tit-bits among the rocks where you thought you couldn't be spotted! He's plain enough now, hung up by the gills: but look, the hook's bare, and he has swallowed the fig and the gold into his guts.

CANDOUR: Make him disgorge, by Zeus, so we can bait for others. Good! What do you say, Diogenes? Do you know who this fellow is? Any connection with your outfit?

DIOGENES: None at all.

CANDOUR: Well, t'other day I put him down as worth about twopence. What price should we put on him?

DIOGENES: That's too much. He's uneatable, ugly, tough and worthless; throw him head first down the rocks and try another cast; but mind your rod doesn't break under the strain.

CANDOUR: Never fear, Diogenes, they're a lightweight variety, lighter than sprats ... But look! What's that flat-fish? He's coming up like a fish cut in two—a sort of plaice—opens his mouth and swallows the hook. Hoist him up! What is he?

EXAMINER: He calls himself a Platonist.

PLATO: Scoundrel!

CANDOUR: You too looking for the piece of gold, eh? What do you say, Plato? What'll we do with him?

PLATO: Fling the blighter off the same precipice! And let the line down for another.

APPENDIX
LANDSCAPE IN CLASSICAL
ART

In introducing the selection of passages depicting landscapes (Ch. II) we identified three categories of literary landscape: the untamed wilderness, the abode of Pan or Faunus; the man-made pattern imposed on the natural landscape by settlement and cultivation; and finally the extravagant artificial landscapes described by Statius. Here, by way of introduction to the Plates, we shall examine some of the surviving landscape representations in detail, with an eye particularly to their relationship, if any, to our literary landscapes on the one hand, and to the actual patterns of landscape on the other. On a broader front, we shall also be looking at the ways in which country life and country folk are depicted in art.

Representations of landscape and country life have survived in considerable quantity, and in three different media: mural paintings, floor and wall mosaics, and relief sculpture. No original Greek works have so far come to light, and the question whether and to what extent the surviving Roman works are to be regarded as originals or copies of lost Greek originals has given rise to much fruitless debate. All three of our literary categories are represented also on the artistic side; there are many floor and wall mosaics of fine quality, containing vigorous representations of the varied activities of farm and steading, complete with vineyards, olive groves, agricultural workers engaged in ploughing, sowing, watering horses, digging, hoeing, harvesting. Cattle, sheep and goats appear, as well as barnyard fowls and ducks. Hunting scenes are also to the fore, and they are well furnished with a variety of glens and rocky outcrops, forming a suitably wild background to the chase (see e.g. Pl. 4). The overwhelming majority of the mosaics come from Roman Africa, and both natural and man-made landscapes are represented. Artificial landscapes, on the other hand, are almost entirely confined to mural paintings; and for these by far the richest sources are the buried towns of Pompeii and Herculaneum, whose upper- and middle-class citizens freely adorned the walls of their town houses (and sometimes their country houses in the neighbourhood) with murals executed in an astonishing variety of styles and subjects, the latter including mythological scenes, with or without landscape backgrounds, and artificial landscapes of a very peculiar type known collectively as 'sacro-idyllic'. Many of these paintings are still to be seen *in situ*, thanks to the abandonment of the former habit of taking them off the walls of the houses and setting them up in the rather unsuitable environment of the National Museum at Naples. In mosaic, the largest collection by far is now housed in the Bardo Museum in Tunis, while outside North Africa, the most important examples of life in the countryside are those recently uncovered in the Great Palace of the Emperors at Istanbul.

How artificial is the landscape represented in Pl. 6 (the Villa Albani landscape)? Do the quaint and bizarre contents of a 'sacro-idyllic' landscape such as that depicted in Pl. 1 (the Boscotrecase landscape) have any identifiable connections with real classical landscapes, or should they be regarded as an ancient counterpart to the work of Salvador Dali? Have we any means of determining what a real classical landscape looked like? The search for answers to these questions takes us first of all into the area of ritual and belief.

To the ancient Greek, and, to a lesser extent, to the ancient Roman, nothing was profane. His world was full of gods, whether of broad, extended authority like Zeus and the major Olympians, or of more restricted range, like the local nymphs of groves and springs, whose worshippers showed their gratitude for favours received by decorating well-heads or boughs with flowers or fruits (e.g. Ch. VIII l). The implications, so far as the physical environment is concerned, are obvious; the populated centres were filled with memorials of divine activity, where the devout might pause to pray or offer sacrifice; acropolis and agora, citadel and forum, were cluttered with altars and shrines, dedicated to the gods and heroes who protected the citizens; and out in the countryside, the roads and tracks that linked the cities and towns abounded in wayside shrines— as they still abound in Greece and Italy today—shrines to Hermes, patron of travellers, or to Faunus or Silvanus, gods of the woodland, of untamed nature (Ch. VIII k and l). It is against this background that we must look for the answers to our questions.

The African mosaics depicting rural life can be taken as authentic, with everyday activities being carried out by real people; the artist, whether presenting the lady of the manor receiving first-fruits from her tenants (White, *RF*, Pl. 2) or field hands sweating under the broiling sun (Pl. 18), appears to be working directly from life. The Campanian painted landscapes, on the other hand, exude a quite different atmosphere. Some have an 'impressionist' flavour; others could perhaps be labelled 'romantic' or 'enchanted', for example, the river scene depicted on the wall of a villa on the Appian Way, south east of Rome, and now in the Villa Albani (Pl. 6). In the left foreground is a bridge of the 'pack-horse' type over a stream, consisting of a barrel vault, surmounted by a parapet. The approach nearer to the spectator consists of a flight of shallow steps, up which a traveller, equipped with knapsack and walking stick, is making his way, while at the crown of the arch can be seen three cows peering over the parapet, as they are driven over the bridge by a cowherd. Other cattle can be seen wading in the shallows. In the right foreground is a narrow spit of land with a number of figures (cowherds), two of whom are standing in the shade of a sacred tree, which has votive objects draped on its branches, the others are seated. In the centre background are two river craft, one of which appears to

be anchored in midstream, while its occupants engage in fishing. The upper
register contains two substantial single-storey buildings, backed by hills fading
into the distance.

The first impression left by these Campanian paintings is that they are works
of the imagination. One of the best known of the genre, a fresco from the villa
of Agrippa Postumus at Boscotrecase, and now in the National Museum,
Naples (Pl. 1), appears to have been deliberately executed in a romantic style, 'bringing first-century Pompeii close to eighteenth-century England'
(Wheeler, *Roman Art and Architecture*, 1964, p. 197): shrines and other buildings
appear jumbled together in the background, with sacred trees to left and right,
rising straight out of colonnaded enclosures. The centre of the field is domin-
ated by a tall tree in full leaf; in front of it rises a tall, slender column, topped
by a 'Grecian' urn. The foreground is occupied by a small herd of goats, moving
about or resting on a pavement backed by columns, altars and trees, while the
goatherd, a distinctly idyllic figure in the style of conventional pastoral, plays the
lyre and leans elegantly against the podium of another column topped also
by an urn.

An even more consciously romantic flavour is conveyed by another mural
from Pompeii, now in the National Museum at Naples (Pl. 5). Here the principal
feature is an architectural assemblage, consisting of a high platform of marble,
broken away at the front, on which are set two quite separate and extremely
elegant doorways, each framed by a slender pair of columns of the Tuscan
Doric order, the plain architraves surmounted by dentilled cornices, and crowned
by a pair of incurved acroteria, with a delicately scrolled cornice in the centre.
As in many an eighteenth-century folly, the doorways are mere façades, leading
nowhere (at least from the architectural point of view!); what they do lead to is
a theatrical-looking backdrop, consisting of a tree backed by a great amphitheatre of rock; to the left can be seen in the foreground a white goat, peering
over the edge of a chasm; towards the centre a scantily clad man walks behind
another goat with his hands on its back (?), while high up on the right of the
picture other goats are seen clambering up the rocks.

The atmosphere of the last two examples suggests an affinity with the Sicilian
pastoral introduced in the third century B.C. by Theocritus (see Introduction to
Ch. II, p. 25), and later imitated by Virgil in his *Eclogues*. The architectural
elements, which include elaborate raised platforms and two-dimensional façades
are strongly reminiscent of stage settings. A rather less artificial, less 'stagey'
atmosphere pervades the series of delightful murals of late Republican date
(*c.* 25 B.C.) found in the subterranean sepulchre (*columbarium*) of the Villa
Pamphili, Rome, and now in the Terme Museum (see Pl. 7). Though less
artificial in style than the 'romantic' landscapes discussed above, they nevertheless derive their inspiration from the Alexandrian pastoral tradition, but in the
more natural, authentic form to be found in Theocritus' Seventh and Tenth
Idylls (see Ch. VIII c and Ch. IX b). A third, or 'impressionist' category, can
also be identified in the Campanian series. It includes one masterpiece, the

Entry of the Trojan Horse, from Pompeii, now in the National Museum at Naples (Wheeler, 1964, no. 180 p. 195). Here the foreground is occupied by the doom-fraught horse and the straining bodies of the men engaged in dragging it inside the walls, and the central area by a wildly jubilant crowd of Trojan spectators. It has been suggested that the painter who has so brilliantly wedded the landscape and the story may have been drawing on some personal experience of one of the nocturnal fêtes that took place periodically at Pompeii. This remarkable composition leaves the spectator with the impression of a highly gifted artist transferring to a mythical context a deeply felt experience. That he was also influenced by Virgil seems inescapable.

SELECT BIBLIOGRAPHY

The following books and articles have been of considerable value in the preparation of this book:

GENERAL
J.-M. André, *Recherches sur L'Otium romain*, Paris, 1962;
    L'Otium dans la vie morale et intellectuelle romaine, Paris, 1966.
P. Brown, *Roman Society in the Age of St Augustine*, London, 1971.
V. Ehrenberg, *The People of Aristophanes*, London, 1951.
M. I. Finley, *The Ancient Economy*, London, 1973.
L. Friedländer, *Roman Life and Manners under the Early Empire*, tr. by J. H. Freese et al., London (repr.), 1965.
J. Gagé, *Les classes sociales dans l'empire romain*, Paris, 1964.
W. E. Heitland, *Agricola*, Cambridge, 1921.
A. H. M. Jones, *The Later Roman Empire*, Oxford, 1964.
N. Lewis and M. Reinhold, *Roman Civilization*, London, 1955.
R. MacMullen, *Roman Social Relations*, New Haven and London, 1974.
L.-H. Parias (ed.), *Histoire générale du travail: prehistoire et antiquité*, Paris, 1959.
M. I. Rostovtzeff, *Social and Economic History of the Hellenistic World* (2nd ed.), Oxford, 1953; *Social and Economic History of the Roman Empire* (2nd ed.), rev. by P. M. Fraser, Oxford, 1957.
E. C. Semple, *The Geography of the Mediterranean World in Relation to Ancient History*, London, 1932.
E. Sereni, *Storia del paesaggio agrario Italiano* (2nd ed.), Bari, 1962.
E. A. Zimmern, *The Greek Commonwealth* (5th ed.), London, 1961.

LANDSCAPES IN LITERATURE AND ART
(a) IN LITERATURE
K. J. Dover, Introduction to *Theocritus: Select Poems*, London, 1971.
A. M. Guillemin, *Virgile, poète, artiste et penseur*, Paris, 1951.
F. Klingner, 'Über das Lob des Landlebens in Vergil's Georgica', *Hermes* LXVI (1931), 159 ff.
J. P. Mahaffy, *Social Life in Greece from Homer to Menander* (4th ed.), London and New York, 1888.
D. Pearsall and E. Salter, *Landscapes and Seasons of the Medieval World*, London, 1973.
L. P. Wilkinson, *The Roman Experience*, London, 1975.

(b) IN ART
P. H. von Blanckenhagen, *Römische Mittheilungen*, LXX (1963), 100–46.
A. Maiuri, *Roman Painting*, Geneva, 1953.

Z. Pavlovskis, 'Man in an Artificial Landscape', *Mnemosyne*, suppl. xxv, 1973.

W. J. T. Peters, *Landscape in Romano-Campanian Mural Painting*, Groningen, 1963.

T. Prêcheur-Canonge, *La vie rurale en Afrique romain d'après les mosaïques*, Paris, 1962 (with complete inventory of agricultural, seasonal and hunting mosaics).

C. Schefold, *Vergessenes Pompeji*, Munich, 1962.

Sir M. Wheeler, *Roman Art and Architecture*, London, 1964.

COUNTRY AS SEEN BY THE TOWNSMAN

E. Fränkel, *Horace*, Oxford, 1957.

G. Highet, *Poets in a Landscape*, New York, 1957.

J. P. Mahaffy, *Social Life in Greece from Homer to Menander* (4th ed.), London, 1879.

A. N. Sherwin-White, *The Letters of Pliny: a social and economic commentary*, Oxford, 1966.

FARM MANAGEMENT

H. Gummerus, 'Der römische Gutsbetrieb als wirtschaftlicher Organismus nach den Werken des Cato, Varro und Columella', *Klio* I, pt. 5 (1906).

CALENDAR: SEASONAL OPERATIONS

A. L. Broughton, 'The menologia rustica', *Classical Philology* xxxi (1936), 353 ff.

A. N. Duckham, *The Farming Year*, London, 1963.

H. Stern, *Le calendrier de 354:* etude sur son texte et ses illustrations, *Bibl arch. et hist. de l'Institut français de Beyrouth* lv (1953).

AGRICULTURAL HISTORY

N. S. B. Gras, *The History of Agriculture in Europe and North America*, London, 1925.

J. M. Houston, *The Western Mediterranean World*, London, 1964.

A. H. Slicher van Bath, *The Agrarian History of Europe*, A.D. 500–1850, tr. by O. Ordish, London, 1963.

COUNTRY PURSUITS

(a) CULTS AND FESTIVALS

L. R. Farnell, *The Cults of the Greek States*, 5 vols., Oxford, 1896–1909.

W. Warde Fowler, *The Roman Festivals of the period of the Republic* (2nd ed.), Oxford, 1908.

Sir James Frazer (ed. and tr.), *The Fasti of Ovid*, 5 vols., Oxford, 1929.

M. P. Nilsson, *Greek Popular Religion*, New York, 1940.

(b) PRIVATE PLEASURES

J. P. V. D. Balsdon, *Life and Leisure in Ancient Rome*, London, 1969, Chs. IV–VIII.

L. Casson, *Travel in the Ancient World*, London, 1974.

J. H. d'Arms, *Romans on the Bay of Naples*, Cambridge, Mass., 1970.

A. Foucher, 'Cicéron et la nature', *Bull. Ass. G. Budé*, 4th ser., III (1955), 32–49.

A. G. McKay, *Houses, Villas and Palaces in the Roman World*, London, 1975, Ch. V.

Evelyn, Countess Martinengo-Cesaresco, *The Outdoor Life in Greek and Roman Poets*, London, 1911.

G. Steiner, 'Columella and Martial on living in the country', *Classical Journal*, L, pt. 2 (1954), 85–90.

HUNTING AND FISHING

J. Aymard, *Essai sur les chasses romaines*, Paris, 1951.

S. Barthelemy and D. Gourevitch, *Les loisirs des romains*, Paris, 1975.

A. J. Butler, *Sport in Classical Times*, London, 1931.

Note: for more detailed discussion of the technical aspects of farming covered in Chapters V and VI, the reader may refer to my *Roman Farming*, London, 1970.

INDEX OF PASSAGES

GENERAL INDEX